Learning Jesus

Learning Jesus

STEPHEN D. JONES

Foreword by Jennifer W. Davidson

RESOURCE *Publications* · Eugene, Oregon

LEARNING JESUS

Resource Publications
An Imprint of Wipf and Stock Publishers
199 W. 8th Ave., Suite 3
Eugene, OR 97401

www.wipfandstock.com

PAPERBACK ISBN: 978-1-6667-1195-0
HARDCOVER ISBN: 978-1-6667-1196-7
EBOOK ISBN: 978-1-6667-1197-4

09/21/21

Dedicated to My Parents,
Dwight L. and Elizabeth R. Jones,
From whom I learned Jesus

And as the child grew to maturity, he was filled with wisdom, and God's favour was with him.

—LUKE 2:40, NJB

And as Jesus continued to grow in body and mind, he grew also in the love of God and of those who knew him.

—LUKE 2:52, PHILLIPS MODERN ENGLISH

Contents

Foreword by Jennifer W. Davidson   ix

Introduction   xi

Chapter One | Stories of Jesus Learning   1

Chapter Two | Jesus as a Learner   45

Chapter Three | Learning Jesus   122

Bibliography   129

Foreword

By coincidence, I happen to be writing this foreword to *Learning Jesus* the same week that I am enrolled in a workshop at the Stanford Life Design Lab. The workshop is filled with higher education professionals—deans, career counselors, and professors like me—who want to bring the insights from the Life Design Lab into our universities and graduate schools. We've signed up for the workshop because we have read the books and other materials, engaged with and loved the ideas we found there, and are excited to teach it to others. But the folks at Stanford wisely organized the workshop so that, for the first two of the five days, all the participants are asked to be learners *only*. "Take off your teacher or administrator hat," they told us. "And experience this curriculum as a learner and designer of your own life. This felt experience," they assured us, "will inform your teaching."

It is a vulnerable thing to assent to be a learner. It means admitting that we do not know yet what we need to know—or do not know how to do what we need to do. Admitting that we do not know something can be a frightening thing to do. It can make us feel inadequate, uncomfortable, and apologetic. Paradoxically, the farther one gets in the education system in the United States, the less conducive the classroom environment can be for learning. Too many of our classrooms are set up for students to prove what they know. Teachers award the highest grades to the students who speak with the most certainty. Unfortunately, this can even be true for some classrooms in theological seminaries.

Love for learning thrives in spaces where students are allowed to admit what they do not understand. A commitment to lifelong learning grows when students are invited to explore the very edges of what they think they know. Teachers who remember what it is like to be a beginner at something will bring compassion to the classroom. Assenting to be a learner isn't less frightening in compassionate classrooms, but the learner feels bold and brave enough to enter the unknown.

In the courses I teach, students do not give final presentations on their projects. They give presentations on their works-in-progress before their projects are due. This is an intentional pedagogical move, because I want to undermine the tendency in higher education for scholars to present their finalized thoughts on a topic with their tersely worded theses and intricately woven arguments. I remind my students that when we only present our final projects (our final thoughts), it leaves the audience with the impression that the road was smooth, the ideas were always fluent, and the thinking on the subject has been completed. But when we present works-in-progress, we invite people into our process of learning, we ask for help where we all (inevitably) struggle, and we remind ourselves that no thinking should ever be final. We need to engage one another and get out of our own heads so we can keep on learning.

That is why *Learning Jesus* is such a refreshing book. What a comfort it can be to know that Jesus, too, made himself vulnerable enough to be a learner. And if we are to imitate Jesus, as I believe we are, then what a liberating idea this is! We need not prove what we know to God as if God were the terrifying teacher with a red pen and gradebook in hand, marking down each of our mistakes with a cluck of the tongue. No! Instead, we can hear compassionate exclamations of delight, as if God were saying, "Well, that was an unexpected tumble! Tell me, what do you think you might learn from that? What else does that make you want to learn? Let's do it together!"

In the pages that follow, you will encounter Jesus again through the re-telling of some key moments in Jesus's life when he was a learner extraordinaire. You may also have moments of sheer delight when you discover that some of Jesus's greatest insights were nuggets of wisdom he learned from his Mom. And you may, if you are lucky, be brought to the edges of what you thought you knew—and find yet another opportunity to learn anew.

Jennifer W. Davidson, PhD
Berkeley, California

Introduction

I have written two books on Jesus as a teacher. The first book was entitled, *Rabbi Jesus. . .Learning from the Master Teacher.*[1] I explored five teaching styles of Jesus as a Charismatic Teacher, a Subversive Sage, a Transforming Teacher, a Lover of Questions, and a Risen Rabbi. My second book was entitled, *PeaceTeacher: Jesus' Way of Shalom.*[2] I followed Jesus' life-stages as the Gospels present him as the Anticipated PeaceTeacher, the Compassionate PeaceTeacher, the Lenten PeaceTeacher, and the Resurrected PeaceTeacher.

Clearly, Jesus as a teacher has been very important to my understanding of him. Yet, many scholars, preachers, and Christians have minimized Jesus as teacher, as if it detracts from his role as Savior. New Testament scholar Marcus Borg summarizes his issues with viewing Jesus primarily as a teacher by saying, "The problem with 'Jesus as teacher' is not that it's wrong, but that it's shallow."[3] I take serious issue with this critique. The only thing shallow about Jesus as teacher is if we limit the role to the first century. Jesus is still the teacher of the church and of his followers today.

It was over ten years ago when this question captured my attention: "Was Jesus a learner?" I realized that my focus had been upon Jesus as a teacher, but I had never asked or explored whether he was a learner. It has been a question that has enthralled me for the past decade. I first discovered that the two foci are integrally related, as teaching and learning always are. And then I discovered that Jesus as a learner raises many interesting core

1. Peake Road/Smyth and Helwys, Macon, Georgia, 1997

2. Baptist Peace Fellowship of North America, Charlotte, North Carolina, 2011

3. Borg, *Jesus, Uncovering the Life, Teachings and Relevance of a Religious Revolutionary,* 14.

questions as to his identity and calling. We will explore these in the second chapter of this book.

Yet, there is one abiding related truth: *great teachers are first great learners*. Teachers aren't just scholars who have mastered the facts; they teach their students the love of learning—something one can only teach if first personally experienced. There are no exceptions. Jesus wasn't just a Wise Sage who couldn't be bothered with students. That is why he said to his disciples, "You are all students." (Matt. 23:8) And why he grew so excited when his disciples showed evidence of learning. (Matt. 16:17)

The greatest teacher in my young years was Jim Ward. He taught English and drama in my high school. He was an imaginative, demanding, and insightful teacher. And nothing brought out his love of learning more than halfway through his senior World Literature Class as he introduced the novel, *The Brothers Karamazov.* He became animated and excited as he introduced this Russian author to a group of high school students from the Ozarks, during the height of the Cold War, no less! One of the most outstanding early experiences I had as a student was later in that semester, after we had moved on, when I was with Mr. Ward in a setting outside school. I don't recall what happened but I likened the experience to one that happened in the Karamazov book and offered my insight about it. You would have thought I had just revealed one of life's deepest secrets. Mr. Ward was so excited because as teacher and student we could enjoy, for a brief conversation, a more level playing field where we could teach and learn together! It is a great teacher who can inspire students in this way—as great learners together! Jesus surrounded himself with such a learning community!

If Jesus was an amazing teacher, did he not also have to be an amazing learner? This led to the question: Do the Gospels depict Jesus as a learner? Do the Gospels ever say, "Jesus learned something today"? If not, why would they have hesitated? As I studied the Gospels more closely, I began to recognize assumptions and experiences, here and there, affirming that Jesus indeed was a learner.

Finally, I asked myself: Does this really matter? If Jesus was a learner, is it important? And I have reached the conclusion that it matters a great deal.

The church has had different perspectives on Christology since it's beginning. Certainly Paul's perspective steered the church in a particular direction within twenty years after Jesus' life. Paul focused almost exclusively on Jesus' death and resurrection, while the Gospel writers felt a need to introduce Jesus from his Galilean/Palestinian roots.

I'm wondering if we aren't entering a new era of Christology, one that poses an "Arrived Jesus" vs. a "Becoming Jesus." The differences in these two perspectives are startling in their implications. An Arrived Jesus had already arrived at God's destiny for his life from the beginning. He perfectly followed God's script from the manger to the cross. An Arrived Jesus floats about a foot above the earth.

A Becoming Jesus had to make the journey. He had to find his way from "here" to "there." He began as a helpless infant. And during his growing up years in Nazareth, his fellow townspeople apparently did not recognize a halo over his head or the emergence of the anticipated Messiah.

Like all of us, the Becoming Jesus had to grow into God's destiny for his life. He had to make choices, he had to unlearn some biases that were part of his Nazarene upbringing, he had to cross barriers and boundaries, until, he was finally able in the midst of his ministry to embrace what God was calling him to do and be.

The title of this book affirms this: there was a "learning" Jesus, just as there was a teaching Jesus. But it also has a second meaning I will explore at the end of this book: we aren't called to be experts on Jesus' life, but we are called to "learn Jesus." It is no longer an adjective but now a verb. And the way we learn Jesus is absolutely unique to Christianity.

I begin by telling stories, as if in Jesus' own voice, about 27 experiences of his life and what he learned from them. These stories are best if read or told out-loud. Through stories we can more easily discover Learning Jesus—in both meanings of the term.

STEPHEN JONES
Kansas City, Missouri

Chapter One

Stories of Jesus Learning

First-person stories, told from Jesus'
perspective, of events from the four Gospels
that reveal his pilgrimage as a learner.

Jesus' mother treasured all these things in her heart.
—LUKE 2:51B

My Home Had a Secret

My home had a secret. A well-kept secret. I'm not sure how old I was when I became aware of it. I guess old enough to learn not to speak of this with my friends in the village of Nazareth. You must understand that keeping a secret in a small village is really a challenge! Everyone knows everyone else's business. Your missteps are the conversation of the village for weeks. And every child has missteps growing up. It's how you learn. It's how you mature. It's how you grow. It's humanly impossible to painlessly navigate every crossroad or challenge.

I think this secret held in our little trio in our home, mom, dad, and me, likely delayed my parents having another child, for my next oldest sibling, James, was born seven years later. How would another sibling be added to "the secret"? And since the secret was about me, and about my identity and my calling, how could a second or third sibling be expected to keep it?

My father wasn't a big talker. He was good with his hands. He was the village carpenter. He could build or design anything. When working, he spoke few words and didn't like to be interrupted. I asked lots of questions. It was his deep desire that I learn from him, so that I could take over the carpentry business. So, he conversed with me more than anyone else. But we talked mostly about wood. As my father got older, I was his helper lifting big pieces of wood into place while he honed each piece to his high standards. Nothing was sloppy or mediocre in my father's shop.

So while our family secret was held by my father, he rarely spoke about it with me. That was my mother's role. Everyone in the village respected my mother. I knew that from the youngest age. It was obvious in the way women and men interacted with her. Had the synagogue been a place where women could vocalize their faith, my mother would have been a leader. Instead, she found ways to express her faith behind the scenes, with other women, but even, in private, with men in the village whom she trusted and even more important, who trusted her. Many neighbors regularly sought her counsel. Eventually, my mother became a de facto spiritual leader in Nazareth. It was better that no one stated this out-loud.

It didn't surprise anyone that I showed spiritual aptitude from my earliest years. No one would expect anything less from Mary's son. My mother would sing psalms while washing clothes, sweeping the house, preparing meals—she seemed to be praying or singing psalms unceasingly. She never did it for show. My father and I were the only ones to see the depth of her devotion to God. She taught me, "When you pray, Jesus, go into your room and shut the door and pray to your Father who is in secret; and your Father who sees in secret will reward you." (Mt 6:6) Throughout my life, I followed my mother's example and found private places to pray.

Nazareth was an out of the way village and people rarely traveled through Nazareth. King Herod was building one of his new cities from the dirt up just a few miles down the road from us. And that is where all the action was. Not in Nazareth.

We Nazarenes kept to ourselves and turned our back, as best we could, on Herod's designs down the road. We did not want to be corrupted by his worldly influences.

Our ability to turn inward was how our family kept our secret. My mother told me, "Jesus, at your birth, your father and I separately had visions, like a visit from an angelic messenger." I naturally exploded with questions, dozens of them, but mother was measured with her answers. And always, whenever she would reveal anything about my birth, she would remind me of our family secret. "Tell no one," she would say. I would respond, "But, mother, if what you are saying is true, isn't this wonderful? Isn't God awesome? Won't my friends want to know?" And she would look sternly at me. "Wonderful? Yes, Jesus. Awesome? Yes our God is awesome. But tell no one, Jesus."

"Mother," I asked one day, "is it good to keep this a secret?" She responded, "Nothing is hidden that will not someday be disclosed, nor is anything secret that will not, in God's good time, come to light." (Luke 8:17) She continued, "But if we testify about ourselves, it seems we are seeking honor for ourselves. Rather, in good time, you will seek to honor God with your call." (John 7:18)

As I got older she explained why my family kept this secret. She said, "People in our village would resent it if they felt you were more special than other children. They would resent our family. They would pick on you and you would be miserable. It's for your own protection, Jesus. I want you to have a loving childhood in a normal home, even though God has extraordinary plans for you. Of that, I am certain. And in God's good time, when your Father in heaven knows you are ready, then you will begin your public ministry. But only in God's good time, Jesus, not ours." Another time she spoke again, "Right now, your work is to learn the Torah. Learn it well. As the prophet Jeremiah said, 'I will put my law within them and I will write it on their hearts, and I will be their God and they will be my people.' (Jer 31:33b) But even more important, Jesus, learn God! Learn about your heavenly Father. Learn to speak with him. Learn to listen to him. You cannot do what God has called you to do unless you and the Father are one."

So, we kept the family secret. James, too, and my other siblings, kept the secret. Mother was amazing at bringing all of them into our circle of trust.

When I became a man, I continued to live in Nazareth and I took my rightful place in the synagogue. I remember the first time I was asked to read from the Torah. And the first time I expounded on it. My father was so nervous because these were roles that made him uncomfortable. He wasn't a strong reader so he was seldom asked.

But the other men in the synagogue were impressed that such a young man had these insights. They would look at each other, and out of my father's hearing they would say, knowingly, "Mary." I was Mary's son. I learned carpentry from my father and faith from my mother. Certainly the ability to articulate, to teach, to ask questions, to seek God in the midst of life's daily realities.

And I grew in wisdom, in stature, and I was held in favor by my fellow Nazarenes (Luke 2:40), no doubt because my family knew how to keep a secret.

Jesus at Twelve (Luke 2:4—51)

There is no more special occasion for a Jewish family than when the first-born son becomes a man. In my day, this is celebrated during the lad's 12th year, assuming he has completed his Hebrew and Torah studies in his local synagogue. And there is no better place for this rite of passage to occur than in the Temple in Jerusalem. They say the Temple is one of the celebrated wonders of the world, glistening in its gold dome in the Jerusalem sun. The first time I saw it, it took my breath away. I had never seen anything so grand. I'd heard the grumblings about Herod who built it, and the many peasants who were taxed so unjustly to raise the funds for it and the many slaves and builders who worked for next to nothing to create it. Still, nearly completed when I was a child, it was a wonder!

On our 12th birthdays, young boys are invited to come to the Temple to meet the scholars of the nation, and to read publicly from the Torah. Fear surpassing all fears, if any scholar decides to ask you a question or to probe your understanding of the Scripture you have read.

When my parents took me to Jerusalem for this occasion, the scholars handed me the book of Genesis, and I read to the elders the story of Noah. Of course, I was nervous. I had never stood before such an impressive group of scholars. There isn't opportunity for anything like this in southern Galilee.

After reading Noah's story in Hebrew, one scholar asked, "Tell me, lad, of what village do you come?" And I responded, "I am Jesus of Nazareth." He responded with a wry smile on his face, "Nazareth? Has anyone here ever been to Nazareth?" Not one hand was raised, but he did raise a fair amount of laughter over the prospect of my coming from such a lonely outpost. He concluded, "No, I didn't think so! So, tell me, Jesus of Nazareth, what is your thought about what you have just read to our solemn assembly?"

I paused just a moment, and then gave him my honest opinion. That's what my father said I should do. I said to the assembly, "I think it shows that God is capable of changing His mind, of relating to mortals in a new way." There was stunned silence.

"God is capable of changing His mind? Is that your response, Jesus of Nazareth? Are you sure of this, lad?"

"You may correct me, to be sure, my Lord. But from what I read, God gave a new promise to those who dwell on earth. God said that He would never destroy the earth again, and He gave us the rainbow as a sign of this promise. Every time I see the rainbow over the skies of Nazareth, I am reminded that no matter how wicked we become or how far we have strayed from God's will, God will not destroy the earth again."

As I was speaking, a growing crowd of scholars walked toward me, encircling me. I couldn't tell whether they were upset by my answer or simply wanted more dialogue. The same scholar asked, "Who taught you these things, Jesus of Nazareth?"

I answered, "Well, no one, really, sir. It seemed obvious from the story itself. God related to us one way up to Noah's time, and a different way after Noah. It was His promise to all of us."

He pursued his question, "But have you not read in the Torah, 'Do not add to what I command you and do not subtract from it, but keep the commands of the LORD your God that I give you.' (Deut 4:2). Another scholar joined him, "And did not the Psalmist say, 'The LORD exists forever; your word is firmly fixed in heaven. Your faithfulness endures to all generations.' (Ps 119:89) Surely you do not believe that the Lord of the Torah and of the Psalms has changed?" He seemed certain to silence me with these thoughts.

I responded, "The Torah of God does not change. The commandments of God do not change. God's faithfulness is constant. But does that mean that God cannot continue to speak to us? Is God doomed to only repeat Himself?"

Another scribe joined in my argument, "This young lad speaks wisely, with amazing insight. God changed His mind in the Garden of Eden, did He not, when the first man and the first woman disobeyed? He responded to their disobedience in a different way than He had hoped!"

Immediately, the entire room erupted in an argument between those who believed that God was changeless and those who argued that God changes as human beings change. Voices raised, spirits were stirred, and I was mostly ignored. I stood there, still in the middle of them, a little stunned. I had never heard such disagreement expressed, so strongly, so passionately. And it went on for an hour before it subsided. I hoped I hadn't said anything wrong.

The original scribe turned back to me, "Tell me, young Jesus of Nazareth, did you intend to stir us up like this? Was this your plan today?"

I know I was flushed, but I answered, "I have never before heard such an argument. I have never been taught in this way in my village in Nazareth." The scholars erupted in laughter. "No," he said, "I suspect that you have not. But you are not disappointed by our questions and our arguments?" I responded, "No, I think it would be the only way to get to the truth. To bring together brilliant minds with strong opinions and express them openly until the truth comes out."

The second scholar who spoke to me asked, "And did the truth come out, Jesus? What did you learn?" I said, "Oh, yes, I learned a great deal. As I said, I've never been a part of such an open conversation before. I have always felt that learning about God is more than memorizing lines from the Torah. It requires understanding what we have read."

One scholar, who seemed to be in charge said, "My, Jesus. How thoughtful are your words. Let us sit together over here, and tone down our argument, and see if in a calmer spirit, we might more deeply probe the truth of God's Word together. Shall we?" Almost immediately, all the scholars formed a circle around this leader and were seated. He asked, "Do you have anything else to say about this, young man?"

I paused. "We believe that God will send the Anointed One to usher in a new era, a new reign where God's will is supreme, do we not?" The kind leader responded, "Yes, we do. That is the hope of the Jewish people." I continued, "And when the Anointed One arrives, will that not be a new Beginning as God speaks to us through the Messiah? And will that not be a change for God and for all of us? Won't the Messiah usher in a New Way?"

There was silence. Not a word was spoken. Not one scholar moved a muscle. My words rang out in the room where we had gathered. Finally, the leader spoke, "And you believe that the Anointed One is coming, Jesus?" I said, "I believe the Anointed One is already here, among us, if we open our eyes and listen with our ears, for God is moving among His people."

The discussion that followed went well into the night. I completely lost sense of time, or how long we had been there. I think the scholars stayed much longer than they intended. We slept awhile, but the next morning, the discussion continued, some time with heated argument and other times with respectful listening. I had never been a part of anything like this. It was wonderful!

I learned from that conversation that faith isn't memorizing words, even sacred words in the Torah. It's learning to probe the deep meaning of the words to understand how God is acting within and among us. It was the most fascinating discussion of my young life, the most satisfying. I didn't want it to end.

And it only ended when my parents entered the room. They were angry with me for not telling them where I was. They had already started back to Galilee, thinking that I had gone on ahead with the other boys. I felt badly to worry them. But the chief scholar walked over to my father and said, "Your son is an amazing boy. I believe that God sent Jesus of Nazareth to us today, for the discussions we've had with him have been a rich blessing. We have learned from his youthful sincerity. I congratulate you on bringing this fine young man to us."

Now, my parents could hardly be angry with me. Just the same, I excused myself and left hurriedly with them. And they had a hundred questions to ask of me about what had just happened. I stored that day in my heart. I learned the joy of searching for God's truth, both in Scripture and in our daily lives. The scribes weren't intimidating at all. They also were seekers after the truth.

What My Mother Knew

My mother was the one who told me about my conception and birth. My father would only confirm her story. He was more talkative about our years as refugees in Egypt. I told him that I felt it was such an exciting story. He stopped smoothing a piece of wood on his workbench, and looked up at me and said, "It wasn't exciting, son. It was dangerous. We were always at risk. But it was the only way we could save you from harm." My father, saving me from harm. Those words were etched in my mind from that day and forever changed the way I thought of him. He was my protector.

My mother first taught me humility. She taught me about my special destiny from God. She loved to tell the story of Hannah and her son, Samuel. And how Hannah promised the Lord that she would give her first born son to the Temple if allowed to conceive.

One night, I was suddenly awakened from sleep. I was about nine years old, and I heard someone calling my name. I went to my parents in the outer room, and they were sound asleep. So, I returned to the room where my siblings and I slept. It must have been a dream. But no sooner was I asleep that again I heard my name, "Jesus."

"Mother," I whispered beside her sleeping mat, "did you call me? Did you call out my name?" She was so sleepy. "No, Jesus, go back to bed and don't waken the others."

A few hours passed—for me to get back to sleep—but again I heard my name, clearer than before. "Mother?" I said. She turned and said, "Did you hear your name again?" I said yes. And she said, "Jesus, take your mat and go up to the rooftop and sleep there tonight." "Really?" I said. "Yes. Go quietly." I loved sleeping up there but only on special occasions was it allowed. Sometimes on the eve of special holy days. It was the first time I slept there alone—certainly not my last.

I quietly carried my mat up the ladder to the roof. I spread out my mat and laid on my back looking up to the heavens. I recalled the words of the Psalmist, "When I consider the work of your hands, O Lord, the heavens. . ." It was as if those words were spoken just for me.

A million distant stars blinked on as I studied the heavens. I was mesmerized by the Wonderful Creative Hand of Yahweh.

It dawned upon me that I was not the first Jewish boy to hear his name called out in the night. I thought of my ancestor, Samuel. "Here I am," I spoke aloud. "I am your servant, your son."

And I heard what could only have been the voice of God. "You are my son, Jesus, with whom I am well pleased."

Humility, as I have said, was my mother's trademark. My disciples once asked why I would say to the people whom I had healed to "tell no one about this." I would smile and say, "I learned that from my mother." And that would end the conversation.

So I held this special calling and destiny in my heart. And mother would drill this into me: "It isn't to make you greater than others, Jesus. You are to be a servant to all others. You were born to me, the least of these. Someday, somehow, God will lift you up. But never ever let this go to your head. Store this in your heart and speak of it to no one. You will be God's instrument of salvation for our people. And someday, everyone will know this. Everyone for generations to come. Jesus," she would continue, "God has chosen you. You did nothing to deserve this and neither did I or your father. It is God's unmerited love. But still, Jesus, know deep in your heart that God's way for you will be revealed in good time."

She always emphasized those last words. I learned so much from her. Sometimes, she spoke with sadness, with a heavy heart, when helping me understand my destiny. I didn't know why. At the time.

Because of her lessons, I hardly ever spoke to anyone of the role God had called me to fulfill. But on the night I heard God call my name, I first became convinced of it. And I knew if others were to see God through me— it would be from my actions, my love, my seeking to be a servant to all. If others wanted to praise God through me, that was their choice. But my mother made sure I knew: never praise yourself.

She taught me well.

My Mother's Prayers

As far as I can recall, I remember my mother's prayers for me. She also prayed for my siblings. It was just her nature. But I believe that her prayers for me were unique, because she was so convinced that the hand of God was upon me. How do I know that she prayed for me? Because I heard her—often! Prayers were spoken out loud through all of her daily tasks. If she was kneading bread, or stoking the fire, or washing clothes, all of these tasks she tended to do by herself, she prayed through it all! Sometimes when I thought about it, it seemed peculiar. Other mothers did not pray out loud like that. But I came to cherish her prayers. They molded my character. They shaped my expectations. I learned so much listening to my mother's prayers.

I remember one prayer in particular. I think I was around 19 years old. And it wasn't clear at that time whether I would remain in Nazareth or leave. My mother didn't know that I was within ear-range of her prayer. But she was cooking and praying—just like her custom. And she prayed,

"This is my prayer, Yahweh, that Jesus' love may overflow more and more with knowledge and divine insight so that he can learn the right path for his life. On the day he launches the ministry to which you have called him, may he be pure and ready to produce a harvest of righteousness that comes from following you, my Lord Sovereign."

I knew that I couldn't yet live up to my mother's prayer. But I knew that living up to her prayer was the reason I was born into this world.

Making an Even Better Friend (Matthew 5:38—42)

Have you ever been in a fight? There were a lot of scuffles and back-alley skirmishes among the young boys growing up in Nazareth. Once a friend shoved me and I fell to the ground. He walked over feeling very proud of his superior strength. He kicked me in the side, really hard. And walked off bragging to his friends. And I was left alone. I walked home and my mother immediately noticed my torn cloak.

I didn't want to tell her, but she finally coaxed it out of me. I told her that I planned to get back at him. He had taken me by surprise and I wasn't ready to punch back. Next time, he'd be sorry that he picked on me. I had my fists clenched, as if ready for my confrontation with him.

Leave it to my mother to ask the difficult questions. "And what would that solve, Jesus, if you punched him back? Isn't Josiah a friend of yours? I thought you enjoyed him." "He was a friend," I told her. "But not any longer. I can't let him get away with this!"

My mother asked again, "And why not? If you decided not to punch him back, what other choices do you have? How else could you respond?" "Well," I said, "I can't ignore it." "Alright," she said, "so don't ignore it. What other ways could you respond? If you punch him back, won't he just punch you back and you'll keep fighting until someone really gets hurt. And then his parents will be mad at me and I'll be mad at them and the entire village will take sides, either your side or Josiah's side. There'll be several versions of who started the fight."

"I could talk to him," I suggested. "Yes, you could," she responded. "And what would you say to him?" I thought for a moment. "I guess I'd tell him that I thought we were friends—real friends. And I was really surprised that he would want to hurt a good friend."

"Jesus, I think that's an excellent place to start. You and Josiah have known each other since you were babies. You've always been close friends. It would be a shame to lose your friendship over one mistake."

Gaining confidence in her approach, I said, "I could say, 'I don't care who is the better fighter. It could be you—it could be me. If I refuse to fight you, we'll never know."

My mother said, "I like the sound of that."

"But I would really miss our friendship. If we became enemies, fighting every time we were together, then we'd be fighting every day because in Nazareth, there wouldn't be a way for us not to see each other every day."

Mother said, "Jesus, violence begets violence. I think that is the point you are making. You and Josiah would become enemies instead of friends. Right now, Nazareth is a community of friends for you. But if you start fighting, you'll make enemies. And living here won't feel as safe or secure."

"Alright," I responded. "I'll talk with him." I walked out and walked directly toward Josiah's house. He was inside with his father. I asked if I could talk with his son. Josiah's first words were, "Jesus, I'm sorry. I was showing off to the other boys. But I don't want to lose you as a friend."

Later, my mother and I continued our conversation. She said to me, "If someone wants to strike you, Jesus, maybe you should let him. And if he hits you on the right cheek, maybe you should turn and offer him the left as well. And if someone wants to take your coat from you, maybe you should offer him your cloak as well. When we become filled with revenge, we're only hurting ourselves. If you won't fight back, as you refused to do with Josiah today, often there's no satisfaction in a one-sided fight. There's really no satisfaction in having an enemy. You've made a friend even a better friend today. I'd proud of you, son. You did the right thing. Don't ever forget the lesson you learned today."

Leaving Home

My father died much earlier than any of us expected. And it required a real change of my plans, a postponement of my dreams. I promised my dying father that I would take care of his wife, my mother, and his family, my siblings. As the oldest child and the first-born son, it was my duty. I had learned the carpentry trade from him and by the time he could no longer work, I was able to take over and keep his customers happy.

But I cannot say I was happy. I kept remembering all that my mother had taught me about my special destiny. I kept remembering that night when God called out my name. And I knew, as long as I remained in Nazareth, I was postponing what God was calling me to do.

Yet, I had this family responsibility. I felt stuck, even though I deeply loved my family. I had a calling and I was not fulfilling it. I could not see a way through.

I learned something during that anxious time of waiting: God had a plan. And all good things would come together as needed in God's good time. I hadn't anticipated my next oldest brother, James. I wasn't watching, though apparently everyone else was.

"Jesus," mother said to me, "what are you waiting for?" "What do you mean?," I asked. "James, your brother, haven't you noticed?" "Noticed what?" "Just watch him over the next week and see what you think." I had no idea what she was talking about. Puzzled, I agreed. And it immediately became obvious that James was more than capable of providing for our family and being an able partner to our mother. I was no longer necessary.

"Well?," mother asked me the first day of the next week. "Yes, I see. James is a natural-born leader. I need to leave, mother." "Don't you think I know that? Don't you think I know that God has a special plan for you, Jesus? I might have a suggestion, though, son. Be sure to be in tune with everyone around you, even your brothers and sisters. Don't be so involved with your responsibilities and thoughts that you forget that people matter. They matter to God and they need to matter to you. All of them. The good people and the people who have wandered far."

"Of course, mother. A good lesson. I've been amazed at watching James, all that was happening right under my nose, and I hadn't noticed. It's time for me to launch my ministry. You will support me?" "Always," she said, with a smile and a hug. "Always, Jesus."

Not so long after, I sat down with my siblings and explained what I must do. The younger ones were crying because they had become dependent upon me to resolve their differences and clean their wounds and help them grow. The older ones were well aware of what I must do, certainly James, but also Simon and my older sisters. And they also knew it was time.

I left soon after. And I knew that I could never begin the next chapter of my life without intense spiritual preparation. I had known John the Baptizer all of my life. He was a distant kin of my mother. And I decided my new pilgrimage must begin with him. Off in the wilderness by the River Jordan, I found him. He was preaching to crowds, and baptizing those ready for repentance. We stayed together for almost two years, talking and sharing.

He was a wonderful mentor to me, a role he took seriously. And then the day arrived when I came to him to be baptized.

"Do you need this, Jesus? Are you sure?" "I am sure, John. I am ready, and I know now I need to be baptized. There is no other way for me to begin what I must do." John said, "I've baptized tax collectors, and harlots, and eunuchs and Pharisees. I never considered baptizing you."

"Well, then, John, this is your day. And it's also God's Day. And it's also my day to turn from taking my father's place in Nazareth, and to stand in my Heavenly Father's place, the place of my spiritual calling."

On that day, I was baptized. And that same voice I had heard before, the same voice calling my name, once again spoke to me out of the heavens after I arose from being immersed in those waters, saying, "You are my son, with whom I am well pleased." This was the right path, no question. The Spirit of the Holy One told me so.

My people have always had a relationship with the wilderness. If you are a spiritual person as a Jew, the wilderness calls out. It is a place of simplicity, a place of stark realities, a place to meet God or at least confront God's absence. It is a place of few distractions.

I went into the wilderness and the next forty days were the most difficult of my young life. I met the Devil Incarnate. From the splendor of baptism, to this? What kind of God would do this to me? I was ready to leave the wilderness after a few days, but I knew that I could not. Only God could lead me out, and the time had not yet come.

Only when I was ready, only when I was purified from within, only when I was truly listening for God, waiting for God, was it time to leave the wilderness. It was a hard lesson to learn. But walking back into Galilee, I knew that my God was walking with me. . .to the end of my life.

Calling Disciples (Mark 1:11—20)

John the Baptizer and I had talked about obtaining disciples. He spoke of how important it was. He was busy baptizing, and some would come to him, to repent and be baptized, and linger with him, and never leave. And eventually, he would accept them as his disciples.

One day, while I was still by myself, I passed through the area where John was working. And as I passed by, he said of me, "Behold, the Lamb of God who takes away the sin of the world! This is he of whom I have spoken."

The next day, two of John's disciples came to me, and followed behind me. And I turned to them and said, "What are you looking for?" They asked me where I was staying, and they accompanied me. It was Andrew. He had almost been sent by John the Baptizer to me. The other returned to John's community.

I said to Andrew, "I do not want disciples to find me, as you found me. I think God is calling me to find them. Will you help me find my disciples? I sense they are waiting for me, and they will know when I come to them." Andrew said, "Come with me to my brother, Simon." And we went, and I immediately knew, Simon would be one of my disciples and I would call him The Rock, Cephas. And these two were fishermen. And we kept walking along the Sea of Galilee. And we met Philip. And we met James and John. And we met Levi, a tax collector, and he completely surprised me. He was ready, and he joined us. We met Matthew, and Bartholomew, and then Thomas and James, and another Simon who had been a zealot and was committed to violence. He repented and turned to peace. All of them Galileans. And then, finally, I added a Judean, Judas Iscariot. And I made him the treasurer of all our funds. He was such a competent organizer.

I wish I could tell you that I planned my meeting with each of them. But it didn't happen that way at all. Maybe I didn't even find them. Maybe I wasn't even looking for them. They were waiting for me. And it was the easiest thing I had ever done. And soon, there were 12 of them, and then more.

Women came. A few were married, most were single. Could we travel together? It wasn't done in my society. It might provoke gossip, but again, I didn't find them. I wasn't even looking for them. They were waiting for me. I wish I could explain the logic of it all. But it wasn't very logical, this motley group. By the world's standards, they weren't very impressive. And others laughed at us because not one of us had credentials, or standing, or honor.

And we journeyed together. Oh. . .and, changed the world.

Cana Party (John 2:1—11)

Uproarious laughter is good for the soul.

The one time I returned home, not so long after I left, was disastrous. I knew that visit to Nazareth broke my mother's heart. And it changed her relationship with the other Nazarenes. She never felt quite at home again in our small village. All her children, my siblings, were approaching adulthood. She began to feel free.

The wedding at Cana was my mother's sister's son, my first-cousin. And she sent my brother, Simon, to find me with a message, "Jesus, this wedding is very important to me and to our family. I expect you to be there. Bring with you whom you must—but please come."

So I came. With my disciples, all twelve of them. We exerted no small strain upon the wedding budget. For a wedding lasted for days, and the host was expected to keep food and wine flowing throughout the festivities.

And then, the wine ran out early. As a guest, I didn't see that as my problem. I'd had enough. But my mother pointed out that my 12 uninvited guests and their habits of drinking and having a good time were partly to blame. "You must do something," she said to me privately.

My mother surprised me that day, knowing, as no one else, that I had the power to lift my relatives out of their shame, and lift my cousin and his bride back to respectability. For when the wine runs out, the party is over and the guests begin to leave—even if the festivities were expected to last much longer.

I love my aunt and uncle –and my cousin—they are such good people: down-to-earth, honest, and humble. To see the terror in their eyes when the wedding of their dreams was breaking up prematurely was painful. I don't know what my mother expected me to do, but she knew I could do something. Turning the jugs of water into the finest wine of the day, I hadn't expected to be doing that. I learned that day the importance of celebrating life. I saw that in my mother's approving look. I saw it in my aunt and uncle's startled but appreciative faces. I saw it in my cousin's stunned look, and in my disciples' approval.

We partied and celebrated life, romantic love, a new marriage, the pos-sibilities of a coming generation, and then, at the appropriate time, we left for my new home in Capernaum. I invited my mother to let my siblings return to Nazareth on their own, and join me in Capernaum. She hadn't yet visited my home, nor had she spent any time with me and my disciples.

The celebrative party had opened our hearts, and it afforded one of the most wonderful times I have ever spent with my mother. She was the center of attention—each disciple clearly desiring time with her. Her wonderful cooking kept the celebrative spirit going. Her presence, her hospitality, her loving spirit was a little bit of heaven on earth. And without the miracle at Cana, it would never have happened.

Back in Cana (John 4:46—54)

Sometime later, I was back in Cana again. I had been in Jerusalem and have stopped over in Samaria. And I passed through Cana, where my relatives lived. I had no more arrived in town when a royal official from Capernaum approached me. He was dressed in his royal attire, and I was put-off by the entourage who accompanied him. He had made the trip to Cana because he heard I was traveling in that area. He asked me to heal his son back in Capernaum.

I have been around royal officials before. They want me to put on a show for them. And so I said to the man, "You people, all you want are signs and wonders. But where is your faith?"

The official was stunned. And I could see that my assumption about him was completely wrong. He knelt before me and said, "Good Teacher, my son is dying back in Capernaum and I know you have the faith to heal him. Please, my Lord." This official had humbled himself before me, and it moved me greatly. I lifted him up to his feet and announced to him, "Your son, back in Capernaum, is now restored to health again. Go home and you will find him well."

The official needed no convincing. He never said, "Are you sure?" He completely trusted me and accepted my word. He turned and raced home, fully expecting that his son would be well. The official was never the same man again. And I learned that if you have met one royal official, you definitely have not met them all!

Zacchaeus (Luke 19:1—10)

Most people have told this story about how surprising it was that I entered this tax collector's home. Have you considered how surprised I was to be standing inside Zacchaeus' home, eating his food, drinking his wine, knowing that just outside the door of his house there was a large crowd questioning my judgment? No righteous Jew would approve of my being there.

And, truth be told, Zacchaeus' was the first tax collector's house I had ever entered. I couldn't believe how he lived. I had never seen such extravagance. And I learned that day that Zacchaeus wasn't a stereotype. He wasn't a category. Nearly everyone thought that "tax collector" said everything you needed to know about this man and his family. I learned something different just by walking into his house and experiencing his hospitality. This man wasn't a stereotype, he was a genuine human being. And while he was unclean and unjust in his dealings with others, he was also hopelessly isolated. He felt condemned by the people he was cheating. And when he spoke of his children, the way they were alienated from others, the way they experienced hatred of his family—it broke his heart. I had never thought about that before.

Zacchaeus found salvation that day, and my attitude toward tax collectors began to change. I remembered back when John the Baptist baptized many tax collectors—he hadn't treated them as stereotypes. He knew their spiritual need.

I learned that day that some tax collectors are hungry for God, yearning to return to their place in the community of faith, and ready to make amends to all they have wronged. It's not true of all tax collectors, of course. But my important learning that day was: it's true of one. It was true of Zacchaeus.

Later, I was able to say, "Behold, the tax collectors will enter the kingdom of God ahead of the self-righteous."

So many religious people try to live by the rules, separated from more worldly folks. I was convinced that I had much to learn from worldly people. I learned from known sinners, prostitutes, tax collectors, simple fishermen, eunuchs. . .

And Yet Another Tax Collector! (Luke 5:27—32)

So, I was feeling better about tax collectors and that required a lot of mental re-programming because of the severe stereotypes I had been taught as a young man. When a tax collectors or one of his agents came to Nazareth, when I was younger, it always put everyone on edge. We knew he had come to take away our money and our possessions. And we had very little of either! So, we looked at tax collectors with utter disgust and contempt. They had sold their souls away to the Romans and acted just as corruptly as the Occupiers. Our normally relaxed and friendly village turned to stone when they came to town. It's hard to "un-learn" things like that, isn't it?

But, after Zacchaeus, my mind was changing. These people were lost and estranged from the rest of society. Nazareth turning to stone when they came to town was the way everyone reacted to them. And nothing else mattered to Jews like our good standing in the community of faith. These men were unwelcome in any synagogue or in the Temple. They were outcasts— almost like lepers. They lived among us but we pretended they did not.

Walking along one day, we came to a tax booth along the side of the road. Everyone walked around the booth with quickened pace and downcast eyes so as not to be singled out for paying more taxes. On this day, I decided to walk over to the tax booth. I looked the tax collector in the face. . .with love. I told him, "I am Jesus of Nazareth." He responded, "I am Levi, and I already know who you are." "Levi," I said. "Follow me."

There was a stunned silence that followed. Not one soul in the street moved a muscle. Levi stood and kept his focus on me. Then he slammed his tax book shut, closed his money box and walked out of his booth. He stood before me and said in the clearest voice, "I will follow you, Jesus of Nazareth. Come to my house. You must meet my family and friends. For we are wealthy people living depleted lives."

I accepted and walked beside him. This made quite a spectacle in the street—a tax collector leaving behind everything to follow a rabbi. And a rabbi accepting an invitation to eat in the house of a known sinner? What's going on, here?

Along the way, Levi said to me, "I am a cousin of Zacchaeus. I want the same joy and love of life which he has received from you. I will do every-thing Zacchaeus did to those I have cheated. But I want to follow you, Jesus. That is why I want you to meet my wife, my children, and my friends. I want them to understand this radical repentance to which you have called me."

That night, I met more tax collectors in one place than I had ever seen in my life. I thought to myself, "Just a week ago, could I imagine myself sitting at this table?" Not one of the other tax collectors followed Levi. But they were all deeply moved by my breaking bread among them and grateful for my accepting love.

I didn't feel any different about their vocation. But I did, for the first time, feel differently about them. And I made a point of spending individual time with each member of Levi's family and each of his tax collector friends at the table. It was, truly, a transformative table fellowship. None of us had ever experienced anything like this.

It was suddenly interrupted by Pharisees who had gathered in the street where several of my disciples were waiting for me. The Pharisees complained, "Why does your rabbi eat and drink with tax collectors and sinners?"

My disciples peered through the open window as I walked over. I said to them, "Those who are well have no need for a physician, but those who are sick. I have not come to spend my time with the righteous, but to call sinners to repent."

I wish I could say that every tax collector that night repented and walked over to the Window of Repentance. Only one did. And his name was Levi. And his life and his household were forever changed.

The next few days Levi began returning the money he had wrongly collected and righted every wrong he had committed. He then went with me into the Temple, a place where he would never have been welcomed. And he placed in the Temple a large gift out of gratitude to God. He knelt beside me in that holy place to pray and give his lost soul to God.

And I knelt beside him. And behind him stood his wife, and his wide-eyed children, and his entire household. It was a new day. A proud day.

Samaritan Woman at the Well (John 4)

I love good conversations. And one of the things I have learned is to never retreat from an opportunity to engage in a soulful conversation. Never allow an obstacle to get in the way. And there are so many things that get in the way of good conversations. Why is that? Why do we allow that to happen? Often the best conversations are the most unexpected ones, or ones with total strangers.

It happened one day when my disciples and I were passing near Samaria. Jews never traverse through Samaria, for Jews and Samaritans have a great mistrust of each other. As Jews, we look down upon the Samaritans, for though they are ancestral cousins, we have gone our separate directions. For beginners, we worship at the Temple in Jerusalem and they on an ancestral mountain. The smallest differences between us have expanded out of proportion.

I was tired that day. I've learned the hard way that if I don't have time alone on a frequent basis, I lose my spiritual focus. Sometimes I go into the mountains alone, early in the day. And other times I send my disciples on just so I can have this time alone. Thomas asked, "Shouldn't one of us stay behind with you?" "No, thank you," I said. "I need this time alone."

I was sitting by Jacob's well, thinking of all the people who live in this region and depend upon this well for their daily sustenance. I felt God asking me, "Could you love these people, Jesus?" Just then, a Samaritan woman approached, as startled to see me, a Jewish man, sitting by her well, as I was to see her in the heat of the day. Visiting the well is the first task of the day for village women. You can't get the daily routines of family life started without water. Going to the well was the most communal moment of the day for women. Without men around, they could carry on great conversations and enjoy great laughter. They came to Jacob's well as much for the conversation as for the water.

Only this woman didn't come for conversation. She came when no one else would be there. One look at her face, her dress, the way she presented herself, said it all. One look at her face and posture and it was as if they broadcast her life story. She had a very hard look, masking a lifetime of hurt. She came for water and wanted to avoid me altogether.

I asked her for a drink of water from her bucket. She knew I was a Jew and she knew that Jews refuse to share common containers with Samaritans. She asked, "Why would you, a Jew, ask a drink of me, a Samaritan woman?" I could tell that men were in the habit of asking favors of her –favors that had nothing to do with water. And that she thought so little of herself as to oblige them.

This woman was unclean, a sinner, a Samaritan, and on all these accounts, I should have shunned her.

But while the woman was beaten down by life, she also had a defiant spirit within her. At first, she was certain that I was mocking her, projecting the way Jewish men would respond to her. She was sure that I was mocking their holy mountain, their way of worship.

I felt none of that. To be honest, she was the first Samaritan with whom I had ever had an in-depth conversation.

She eventually offered me water from the well, but in return, I offered her living water, the kind of spiritual refreshment that includes forgiveness and acceptance.

I learned so much from that conversation. It was a spirited give and take. The fact that I was a Jewish rabbi meant little to her. The more we talked, the more I began to see a beautiful person underneath that harsh exterior. She talked of her father's early death in her life, and how her mother had married her uncle, and how he had treated her terribly as a little girl. She'd had her first baby with him. Her first experience with shame.

She told of shame upon shame, one failed marriage after another, adultery, lies, cheating. It was one sordid tale. Yet, I found none of it disgusting, as she assumed. I kept seeing glimpses of a beautiful and articulate woman whose life had gone so badly.

How could I dislike this woman? Was she not a child of God? Her hard exterior gave way to the most revealing and tender smile.

This woman desperately needed living water, just to keep her from falling from one failed relationship to the next. "Do you want living water, to quench your soul?" Through a surge of tears and an open, broken heart, she repented. She was so tired of her life, so tired of people judging her and scorning her.

I forgave her. Yes, that's right. I forgave her. And in a matter of minutes she was gaining confidence. "Why don't you go to your village and tell the others what has happened to you?" She said, "They hate me. They would never believe me. They would laugh at me."

I said, "I'm not laughing." She thought for a moment. "No, you're not. But you are different." And I responded, "No, you are different, and the people in your village will recognize how different you are. They will see it in your eyes, the confident way you are now holding up your head, the good news that fills your soul."

Just as my disciples were returning with food from the village, they were startled to see me talking with her, and even more startled as she headed back to her village. She turned back to me once more, exclaiming, "Living water! Yes, Lord!" She repeated that all the way to her village.

Within an hour, every last person in that village followed her out to the well. They believed her because for the first time in her life, she believed in herself.

We were no longer Jews and Samaritans, and I learned that day how liberating it is when we get out beyond these awful stereotypes we have of those who are different from us. The village leaders insisted that we remain with them a few days. I had never slept in the home of a Samaritan—and neither had my disciples. And, these Samaritans had never before hosted Jews. That first night, it was as if the differences disappeared. It didn't matter. It was astounding.

That woman and those Samaritans taught me something. "Love your enemies, and do good to those who speak ill of you." There was a revival of God's Holy Spirit in that town. And the person who started it all was this sinner woman. And a great conversation.

A Foreigner? Really? (Mark 7:24–30)

Why did I learn so much from women? Really? In my society, there weren't many opportunities for women and men to interact, except through marriage or family. And in my ministry, I kept meeting the most fascinating women. I think because women often get pushed to the side, they come at life from a different perspective. I was so close to my mother, and I found it easy to relate to women of all kinds.

But I can't say that I had any experience relating to Gentile women. In fact, I'd hardly ever been around Gentile women and I was raised with strong ideas about them, about how inferior they were to righteous Jewish women. I'd never even considered that there might be a faithful Gentile woman. Faithful to what? Certainly not to the God of our ancestors. What would it have been like to talk with a woman so totally unlike the Jewish women I knew? Or even unlike the Samaritan women, because, even though our two peoples hated each other, the truth is, it wasn't hard to imagine a righteous Samaritan woman. They believed in the same God even if they worshipped in different ways. Their Law was so similar to ours.

One day, making my way around the outskirts of the region of Galilee, I decided to go further than we had ever gone before. "Jesus," Peter asked. "Why are we traveling into Syria, far out of the region of Galilee? There are so few Jews in this region."

I didn't feel like getting into a debate with Peter. Truth is, I don't know why I walked so far from my natural base in Galilee. I just wanted to get away. And I knew of a Jewish couple, originally from Nazareth, who lived near Tyre, and they invited me to visit them anytime. Their invitation seemed so sincere. And, no one would expect to find me there. It was the perfect escape. We found their home and they offered us most welcome hospitality. I asked them not to tell their friends and neighbors about my visit. I just wanted to be in their home. And they were the perfect hosts. And no one knew me in Tyre. I enjoyed being an Unknown, just for a few days. I was far removed from my places of ministry.

I didn't even leave their house, but just hunkered down to rest, to pray, to reflect. But even so, the word got out somehow. Maybe it was through one of the servants of this family? Late one afternoon, a woman came into the courtyard of their home, pushing past the gate with little regard. She kept thrusting herself into my friend's home until she found me, reclining at table for our evening meal. The woman was a Syrophoenician, and this was her city. She was in her element, and I was out of mine.

I had never met a woman like her, dressed so differently than the women I had known in my life. She kneeled before me and begged that I cast out the demon that had possessed her daughter. I had not come to Tyre to heal this woman's daughter. I had not come to interact with the native people. I had come to this nice Jewish home in a remote location for a retreat, a getaway, a respite. I had come so no one would ask anything of me.

I told the woman, "I am a Jew, and I have come to feed the Jews, for they are spiritually hungry." I turned away from her, thinking she would go away. She did not. She kept begging. I turned back to her and said, "I have come to save the lost sheep of Israel. That has nothing to do with you or your daughter."

I turned away a third time and again it did no good. The woman persisted. Her accent was so thick, so different from the Aramaic spoken in the villages of my people. She dressed with jewels and clothing so gaudy, she appeared as if in a costume. It was hard to take her seriously. I said again to her, more harshly, "It isn't fair that I take what is intended for the children of Israel and throw it to the dogs." I hadn't intended to speak in that way, but the woman had caught me totally off-guard. Even so, she persisted, "Master, even the dogs under the table eat the crumbs the children drop."

She was obviously an intelligent woman as well as a compassionate mother. She humbled herself before me even when I tried to turn a cold shoulder to her. And the more I turned from her, the more she pursued me.

This time, I turned away from the table and toward her, and I said to her, "Tell me, what is it that you want?" And the woman answered, "My daughter has been possessed of an evil spirit and she knows no peace, no comfort. I cannot watch her toss about in such agony. She is possessed, my

Lord." I persisted, "But you are not Jewish. And I was sent to the lost sheep of the House of Israel."

And she said, "But I believe in your God. I have turned from the gods of my people. They have no power. And I know, if you are God's Chosen One, that you can heal my daughter if you choose." I asked, "Where did you get such faith?" She looked at the woman of the household, my friend, with whom I had been staying. I then looked at the two women, and it was obvious that they were close friends. So, this is how the woman entered the house! She wasn't a stranger at all, but a friend of these faithful Jews. And she knew, deep in her soul, that God could heal her daughter.

"Dear woman, if I told you that your daughter was calm right now, unlike anything you have seen before, that the demon had left her, would you believe?" She looked into my eyes in a most penetrating way. "If you say it is so, I would believe it." "Then go home, for your daughter is healed. You will find her lying calmly on her bed. The demon is gone!"

She rushed toward the door. She returned, and kissed my hand, and then fled out of the house. Everyone in the house was speechless for a few moments.

"Jesus," the woman of the house spoke first. "We are of the House of Israel, and we love our people dearly. But tonight, you have met a very good woman, a very faithful woman, and even though she is not Jewish, she is a child of God. I know her to be a wonderful woman. She is not Jewish, but neither is she a dog, Jesus. She deserves God's love. I believe you were led here to our home by the Spirit of God, all the way to Tyre, not only to heal this woman's daughter. But more importantly, to realize that God's love is for everyone's daughter, everyone's son."

I had come into Tyre thinking little of the Gentiles of that region, even though I had never met them. I had come thinking that I was getting away from my mission. And through this woman, I had learned that these Syrophoenician people, this mother, this possessed daughter, were worthy of God's love. My mission suddenly expanded.

And so did my thinking.

And So Did My Journeying (Mark 7:31—8:10)

I did a lot of thinking before I left that home. Healing that woman's daughter was the right thing to do, I was convinced. And pushing her away had been the wrong thing to do. She was Gentile, but she was as capable of placing deep faith in God as any Jewish woman I had ever met.

I was thinking, to myself, that we would leave this distant retreat and return to Galilee, to the familiar places of my ministry, and, of course, among my people. But, in my morning prayers on our last day in Tyre, I sensed that my journey needed to change. It wasn't yet time to return to my fellow Galilean Jews. So, without telling my disciples, we headed in a different direction. We traveled to the towns of the Decapolis, a long distance away. These were also Gentile areas. I could hear my disciples grumbling among themselves, but I walked on—and they followed.

A deaf man was brought to me. Since he had never heard a word spoken, he also couldn't speak well. And his friends begged that I lay hands upon him. Remembering the deep faith of the Syrophoenician woman, I knew what I had to do. But not wanting to create attention, I led the deaf and dumb man off a distance until we were alone. I put my fingers into his ears, and then I spat on my fingers to touch his tongue. And drawing as much spiritual power unto myself, I drew my breath up to my Heavenly Father, and cried out, *Ephphatha!* And immediately his ears were opened and his tongue was released. He heard everything I said to him and spoke clearly to me in return.

I said to the man, "Return to your home by a different way. Your family will want to give thanks with you. But tell no one how God has blessed you with hearing and speech."

But the man was overwhelmed with joy and though he could hear, it was as if he couldn't hear what I had said to him. He raced back toward the crowd and immediately there was a huge commotion when people realized that he had been healed. They were astounded! One man said, "This Jesus has done everything well. He even makes the deaf hear and the mute speak!"

And that is how the crowd began to swell. The surrounding countryside was a desert, and within the next few days, there were thousands of people who came out to hear me. Thousands of Gentiles. The sight of it was a little unnerving, even fearful, the sight of so many Gentiles wanting to hear me.

So, they came, and I taught, and I healed. It was the strangest thing. The spiritual needs of these Gentiles were identical to the spiritual needs of the Jews. And they listened with as much eagerness as any Galilean crowd I had ever addressed. And I realized that this was where God wanted me to be. And why.

Many came on the spur of the moment without preparations for staying a long period of time. And time flew by, and after three days, their provisions had given out. And yet they remained so eager. And I had compassion on them because I knew their physical hunger had to be great.

I couldn't send them away because they would not have the strength to reach the far-off cities and villages. The crowd had come a great distance. My disciples, sensing my compassion, said, "How can we feed these people with bread out here in the desert?"

I said, "Go out among the people and collect all the bread and fish you can find. Tell them, 'You will be fed.'" The disciples asked warily, "Will they trust us?" I said, "Go." So the disciples went out among the vast crowd, Jews asking hungry Gentiles for all their remaining food. In a miracle of trust, they freely gave and returned with seven loaves of bread and several fish. I instructed the people to sit down. I prayed over the bread, giving thanks for the generosity and trust of the people. I broke the bread and gave it to my disciples. And I divided the fish and it also was distributed among the people.

And all ate and all were filled, and they collected what had not been eaten and there were seven baskets full of food. And I instructed them to make sure the children and the elderly had plenty to eat on their way home. There were nearly 4,000 Gentiles in that crowd. And then I dismissed them so they could return to their villages and homes.

We made our way back to the Sea of Galilee, boarded a ship and returned to the Jewish side of the lake. But my perspective had changed. My sense of mission broadened. God helped me realize the spiritual and physical hunger of Gentiles. And why they now mattered to me, because they first mattered to God.

The Woman Who Broke the Rules (Luke 7:36—50)

I usually try to be on my best behavior when I am in the home of a leading Pharisee. It is always an honor to be in their homes and to receive their hospitality. I learned from the Pharisees as a boy. They were my teachers. They were the leaders of my synagogue in Nazareth. Without them, I would know little about the Torah or about God.

But there are rules of hospitality in our culture. You never enter a home for a dinner party without receiving these customs: a kiss by the host of the home on both cheeks of the guests with a warm embrace; the washing of your feet by a servant or member of the household; and, the anointing on your head with a perfumed ointment. After a long walk in the heat, everything and everyone smells better when the perfumed oil drips off your head.

And one day in Nain, I was asked by Simon, the leading Pharisee of that village, to come to his home that night for dinner. Of course, I accepted his invitation. But first, I taught in the center of the town. I taught about our need to seek God's forgiveness. I taught that no matter what we have done wrong, or how far we have strayed, God stands ready to forgive us and help us turn our lives around. I thought, the more I spoke, that Simon was growing agitated with my teaching. He left early and said nothing.

And when I arrived at his home that night, it was obvious. He did not greet me at the door. He did not embrace me or kiss me. He did not order that my feet be washed or my head be anointed with fragrant oil. He remained seated and motioned to me to recline next to him. With the customary prayers of blessing, the dinner began. It was a fine dinner, but the unusual and even embarrassing start was disconcerting.

It was also disconcerting to the crowd in the street who were watching. Our finest homes have courtyards that open to the street and our dining rooms in these homes are also open to the street. So, it is always possible, when a leading family entertains, that any interested person could stand in the street and listen. But not interrupt.

Of course, in Galilee, I am a person of interest because nearly all the rabbis of our time are from Judea. Galilee is felt to be an out-of-the-way place and no respectable rabbi would come from there. And yet, I did. And the village of Nain was not far from Nazareth and I suspect I might have been the first rabbi to enter the village in anyone's memory. I had brought a young man back from death that morning, and, as I have said, taught for a long time in the village square.

When I entered Simon's house, without the customary greeting, there was a gasp outside in the street, as well as murmurings around the table. Why had Simon invited me over only to treat me with such lack of respect? I immediately noticed this—as did everyone else.

And there was a woman in the crowd. I remembered her from the village square that afternoon. The righteous men of the village surrounded me and I could not get close to the woman. But as I looked into the eyes of the people of Nain, no other set of eyes was more responsive than hers. And the more I spoke of God's forgiveness, the more she responded. I knew from her dress and demeanor and the fact that the other villagers shunned her and held her back at the edge of the crowd that she was a known sinner.

That evening, she would not be held back any longer. She boldly crossed the threshold into Simon's house. She entered the dining hall filled with righteous men. The moment she entered there was stunned silence. I suppose Simon could have evicted her with a mere hand gesture, but I think he wanted to know how I would respond to this surprising woman. She was in tears. Not the kind of tears intended to impress anyone, but the kind of tears that came deep within. I knew my words earlier that day had penetrated her soul.

And she came out of gratitude. First, she let down her long hair. That is something women do not do in public, but only in the privacy of their home and family. It didn't stop her. With her tears flowing, I could feel them washing upon my feet and then drying them with her hair. This obviously was a spontaneous act, because she didn't come prepared with a basin or water or with a towel.

But she did bring an alabaster jar of perfumed ointment, and she anointed my feet with the beautiful fragrance that filled the entire room.

Simon was outraged at the audacity of this woman. It was not her place to extend hospitality to his guests. It was his decision alone. And he had decided to withhold. By her entering his house and acting as if the host of the dinner, it brought shame to Simon.

I pointed it out to him when he objected. "Simon," I said. "When I entered your home, you did not extend the customary acts of hospitality to me. You object to this woman, don't you, yet she has acted in love and respect?"

He said in anger, "She is a sinner. And if you were a true prophet, you would know what kind of woman it is that is fondling your feet and shedding tears over you in such an embarrassing way."

I told Simon a parable about forgiveness. He was too outraged to listen. He was so convinced of his goodness that he could not see his own coldness that night. He could not see his smug pride. He could not see his lack of compassion for me, or for her.

Through the parable, I reminded him that everyone, including the righteous, stand in need of God's forgiveness. And this woman, who had lived a hard and difficult life, and who had wandered far from God, was returning home to God tonight, and was asking for God's forgiveness. I turned to her and said, "Your sins, my sister, are forgiven. And your faith has saved you. Go, now, in peace."

Simon never got over what the woman had done, even after she left. And I learned that night that unless someone wants to receive God's forgiveness, you can't make it happen. You have to admit your own sin, without trying to see the sin in others, even this woman. And when you turn to God in this humility, God will forgive you and then you will learn how to love others.

The woman herself was the parable that night. And from her boldness, I learned so much.

How Stupid to Judge (John 8:3–11)

I was in the temple. I had gone early to pray. And people soon gathered around me and I began to teach. The scribes and elders interrupted. I guess they felt they were in charge of the Temple and they could interrupt as they please. At this early hour, they were filled with righteous anger. You could see their seething anger and it was quite startling. They brought in a woman, barely clothed, and threw her down in front of me. The crowd around me quickly backed away, but watched from a distance. The elders charged, "This woman has been caught in the very act of adultery. Now the Law of Moses commands us to stone such women. What do you say?" I wanted to say, "Where is the man with whom she committed adultery?" I looked around wondering if he was in the circle of the accusers. But I knew they were just using this woman to entrap me in a theological predicament. I looked down at this poor, frightened woman. Her life stood in a balance. I kneeled down to her. I cupped her face in my hands and forced her to look up from her shame and into my eyes. I wanted her to sense my tender love.

I then wrote with my fingers in the sand, the Hebrew words, "Be strong in the Lord." I wasn't sure she could read, but she nodded in acknowledgement and I brushed away the sand with my sandal. I desperately wanted to end this provocation without the woman getting hurt, and I realized that the only way was to stand inside her stoning circle. If she would be stoned, than I would be stoned with her.

Would this work or would this be the day of my demise? To say I had no apprehension would be less than true.

I straightened up and looked at the angry men. They each were holding large rough stones in their hands. Any one of those stones was a lethal weapon. I drew the woman to my side, still kneeling before them, and said, "Let anyone among you who is without sin be the first to throw a stone at her." One man raised his hand, and I merely looked at him, pointed at him, forcing him to answer my statement, and he dropped his stone. For he was not without sin. One by one, the elders dropped their stones and hurried away from their stoning circle.

Finally, I was alone with the woman, and we both sighed a deep sense of relief. I stood her up on her feet and said, "Woman, is there no one here to condemn you? Where are they?"

She said, for the first time with a slight smile on her face, "There is no one, Rabbi."

Jesus said, "Then neither do I condemn you. So, you are free to go, only, from this day on, sin no more." She exclaimed, "Yes, My Lord, Yes!" And she fled the Temple in tears of rejoicing.

An Awkward Sabbath (Luke 5:33—34; Mark 2:18—20; Mark 2:23—28; Mark 3:1—5)

My disciples and I were finding our way together. My discipling community was different in so many ways from the Judean rabbis. I obviously was influenced by John the Baptizer, but John was a very austere and serious man. His no-nonsense way spoke to many people. His unusual dress, his severe speech, fit perfectly into the wilderness backdrop which was the habitat of his ministry. John didn't come to you. You had to find him.

I knew in my heart that God was calling me out of the wilderness. God wanted to me to go into the towns and villages and cities of Galilee as my mission field. These were my people—and I had great empathy for them. I desired to speak to Galileans in their natural habitat—and use language and metaphors they could easily understand. When I first called disciples I wondered, "How will my community be different?"

I knew I hadn't called them to serve me—to cater to my every need. And I didn't want a highly regimented society. I wanted our life together to be based in the spirit of the Torah, based in faithfulness to God's commandments. But was there a way to do this while at the same time basing our life together on liberty? Are these opposites? I wanted my disciples to use their minds and that is why I told parables—to make them think. I wasn't interested in their memorizing dogma—but rather allowing God's Spirit to transform them. I needed that—and I knew they did as well.

I disliked the solemnity of John the Baptizer's group. The years I spent with them were filled with obsessing over the ominous dark clouds that hovered over the disbelieving and unrepentant generation in which we lived. In many ways, John was right. But I wondered, Does it need to be this severe—this foreboding? What about joy? What about laughter? What about celebrating God's Presence all around us?

Could we laugh among my followers as well as shed tears? Could our hearts be filled with gratitude as much as regret? Could our message be joyful instead of severe? There weren't many smiles among John's followers. He himself rarely smiled or laughed. John's preaching and temperament were consistently severe. He was an angry prophet. Maybe our generation needed one.

I wondered, "What would happen if we laughed together—a lot?! What would happen if we based our life together on abundance rather than deprivation? I wasn't against fasting or abstinence. But what if we were known by what we add to our lives rather than what we subtract? Would that speak to others?

Do you, O Holy God, want us to be so serious, so morose, so filled with judgment?

Maybe not.

I loved telling stories and I loved helping people smile and laugh. I loved serving people, helping them get over those huge obstacles that so often stand in our way.

I wanted people to hear God's good news for them—not God's severe news. I wanted them to be drawn to God's kingdom of shalom. I wanted them to come to God out of joy, not fear. I wanted them to dwell on God's good news! The world around us already obsessed on the negative. I don't think God intends to pile on more negativity. I think God intends to un-burden us!

Among my followers, we focused on the weightier demands of the Law. I felt that some Pharisees focused on frivolous issues that subtracted from the Law. I know they are sincere, but it just didn't work for me.

One day, we were walking through a cornfield on the Sabbath. I was walking ahead of them, responding to questions by a new seeker I had just met. And my disciples followed behind. I don't think they thought much about it—but they picked corn from the edge rows of this field and it happened on the Sabbath. (Luke 6:1—5) Some local Pharisees in that area had been watching us from a distance and they immediately came out of hiding to confront those disciples. It caused quite a commotion.

I rushed back to the field. The Pharisees came to me saying, "Why do you allow your disciples to pick corn on the Sabbath? It is a violation of the Law."

I wanted to say, "Really?! We are going to get in a dispute over a few ears of corn on the Sabbath—when the weightier issues of the Law are pressing against us? Really?"

But, I didn't. I paused to recall that such laws on the Sabbath can be set aside for a higher cause and I told them, "Surely you have read what David did when he and his companions were hungry? He entered the House of God and took and ate the Bread of the Presence which it is not lawful for any to eat but the priests?" Of course, they had read it. But it seemed to end the argument. Good enough for David—good enough for us. And cornfields didn't exactly compare to the Temple.

A little later, with the offending disciples still moping about with lowered heads, we gathered to reflect on the day. I began, "That wasn't our finest hour. I am trying to re-focus the Pharisees when they concern themselves with the lighter matters of the Law, and I had to defend your picking ears of corn on the Sabbath. We walked right into their trap."

They started to object. I raised my hand and continued: "I know this is partly my fault. I have not stressed these less important matters because I want my single focus to be on introducing the reign of God into the world. Your picking corn has little to do with that.

"But we are all Jews, and our audience is Jewish. And you know that what you did this morning offends many people. And we've been together long enough for you to realize that someone is always watching us. Are you embarrassed today because you picked corn on the Sabbath or because you got caught? I suspect it is the later." I laughed, and they did as well. That laughter was cleansing.

I continued, "It is important for us to be mindful not to offend people over trivial matters. Of course, keeping the Sabbath is not trivial—not at all. One day a week that we give to worship and praise God, to rest and meditate, and to reflect on all the ways God has been present in our lives over the past week. It's all good. It's a day for taking stock. And this is exactly what we are doing right now as a community: taking stock of the day.

"You'll recall last Sabbath that I entered the synagogue at Bethsaida and began teaching. The Pharisees brought a man who had a withered hand before me. I knew what they were thinking and I asked the man, "Come here and stand." And the man got up and stood before me and all the others. And I asked them, 'Is it lawful to do good on the Sabbath or to do harm, to save life or destroy it?' And no one had a response, did they? They lowered their heads because they had no answer, as some of you did when we came together tonight, right?" Again, we all laughed. Do you recall my asking the Pharisees, "If one of you has a child who has fallen into a well, would you rescue the child on the Sabbath?" (Luke 14:5)

"I restored that man's withered hand on the Sabbath in that synagogue and everyone there was lifted up to the higher calling of the Sabbath: to do good."

John, one of the offending disciples in the cornfield said, "We can do better than this morning. We must keep the focus, not on violating the lesser points of the Law, but on how to reach its ideals." I responded, "Beautifully said, John, and more succinctly, also! Does everyone see the point? Or are you going to make John explain it again?" Again—we all laughed.

What had started as an awkward Sabbath ended up being a beautiful Sabbath as we said our prayers together and sang songs of faith. God had been so good to us. And we all learned a thing or two.

It's Bigger than Any of Us Imagined!
(Mark 9:38—41; Matthew 24:36)

Often religious people think they know and understand so much that they predict God's actions. And this is impossible. Or they think we already know what God is up to. And that also is impossible. No one can predict God. No one can fully know God's way. That's my issue with so many of the Pharisees: they believe they alone know what God desires.

One time John came up to me and reported what to him was a most disturbing bit of information: "Teacher, we saw someone casting out demons in your name, and we tried to stop him, because he's not one of us."

Do we really think that God only works through certain people or certain groups? Can we believe that God even works through those who fully deny him? Maybe a little earlier, I might have grown concerned like John, thinking, "We've got to keep this movement within our control. We can't allow anyone to take our place or distort our message."

But I've witnessed God doing incredible things. I've seen God at work through tax collectors. I've heard God speak through a Samaritan woman well known as a sinner. I've witnessed God at work through a Syrophoenician woman. I've seen unsuspecting folks play a role in God's plan they couldn't possibly have understood.

God has broadened my perspective and widened my view. So I said, "John, don't try to stop him. If God is using him, we won't be able to stop him anyway. And if he is a fraud, that's God's role, not ours, to correct him. Whoever is not against us is for us."

The moment I said that I wondered, "Is that really true?" The more I thought about it, the more it rang true. God can use anyone and they don't have to be a part of our inner circle, or our following. It's bigger than anyone of us imagined.

As hard as I try to be in tune with my Heavenly Father, there are limits to what I understand. I believe that God will bring human history to an end, but only in God's good time. I once said to my disciples, "But about the day or hour no one knows, neither the angels of heaven, nor the Son, but only the Father."

Don't Expect Me Back (Mark 8:27–30)

I took an evening stroll outside Capernaum. I often enjoyed walking by myself, without followers or crowds. It required that we provide some distraction so people crowding around me would look the other way and I could make my escape. And just get away. When everything was going right, I went to the mountains. And I often told my disciples, "Don't expect me back." I'd spend the night. It not only gave me time to think, but it also gave me time to listen to God. To allow God to instruct me, to fill me with blessed insight. Those times were too rare but always pleasurable.

But on this particular evening, I walked outside Capernaum, and I sat on a lakeside hill and just watched the beauty of the stars, the moon, reflected on the still Galilean water. And I was ready to return home. No one knew where I had gone, and most didn't know I had left home. As I came into the city, I heard loud conversation ahead of me. I ducked behind a corner to listen. To my surprise, I was the topic of the heated conversation. They were debating who I was: not my sincerity, but my role. One man was arguing that I was Elijah and another was arguing that I stood in the role of John the Baptist. And neither man gave an inch. And I wondered, is this what people talk about when I am not present? I'm not sure anyone feels comfortable being the topic of conversation. So, I turned, went another way, and reached my home unnoticed. My disciples had gathered and were waiting for me.

I wondered, what would they think? So I asked them. "I just came around the corner a few blocks away and I heard this crowd debating about me, about who I am, about my role in God's destiny. Have you heard this? Have you heard crowds talk about me? What have you heard them say about me?"

My disciples had heard these conversations and I was surprised it had never come up among us. "Some say you. . ."

That was quite informative. Then, I wondered, "But you, who do you say that I am?" As with any piercing question like this, that requires self-revelation, "What do you think of me?" There was a long, thoughtful pause. I had no idea how they would respond. And then Peter said it, "You are the Messiah, the Living Christ." Yes, they all agreed, that is exactly what you are to us.

I guess my confusion and theirs was understandable. I had never taught them, "I am the Messiah, the Living Christ." When I spoke, I used a metaphor, the Son of Man. You'll recall my mother teaching me humility? I didn't like to go around making self-pronouncements.

John once sent his disciples to me asking, "Are you the Messiah? Or should we be looking for another?" Rather than answer their question directly, I said, "Go and tell John what you have seen and heard."

Hearing my disciples speak those words for the first time, I realized if they began proclaiming it we would hasten the end of my life far ahead of God's timing. The authorities in Jerusalem would go directly to the

Romans and say, "We have someone out there proclaiming that he is our new leader. The Messiah will lead a take-over of the government and re-establish Jewish autonomy. He will organize a group of Jewish terrorists to take back the land."

So, I told my disciples, "I will confirm, you are right. But this is not the time to publicly proclaim this. You will have that moment in time. But for now. . ."

Learning to Pray (Luke 5:33—39)

One day, a group of earnest and righteous men came to me and asked, "John's disciples frequently fast and pray together. And so do the followers of the Pharisees. But you do not. Indeed, they say of you, 'John the Baptist has come eating no bread and drinking no wine, and some say, "he has de-mons." But of you they say, 'Look, a glutton and a drunkard, a friend of tax collectors and sinners.'"

Once again, I was being compared to John's austerity and severity. I deeply respected John—but I had my own way that differed from his. And so I told this group a parable, "And no one puts new wine into old wine-skins; otherwise the new wine will burst the skins and will be spilled, and the skins will be destroyed. But new wine must be put into fresh wineskins. And no one after drinking old wine desires new wine, but says, 'The old is good.'" (Luke 5:37—39)

I didn't elaborate. I rarely did with parables. That's the point of them: you want people to think. What does this parable mean? Why did he tell it to me? Anyway, it silenced them and I suspect it forced them to ask these very questions. But later, reflecting alone with my disciples, they also questioned me. And I said to them, "You cannot make wedding guests fast while the bridegroom is with them, can you? The days will come when the bridegroom will be taken away from them, and then they will fast in those days." (Luke 5:34—35) They look puzzled, so I continued, "The day is com-ing when I will no longer be with you. For what we have started together will not end without a great confrontation between Good and Evil, between Truth and those clutching to the deceit of this world."

Silence followed. So I asked them, "What of you—do you think we should fast together, abstain together, and pray? Do we have too much fun?!" We all laughed.

Thomas said, "I know John's disciples have been taught by him how to pray, and they recite a common prayer every morning and evening. I know you want us to pray in our own words and honest feelings. But could you teach us a Followers Prayer, something we could repeat and find a deeper connection with God?"

I said, "It is a thoughtful request, Thomas. Let me ponder what you have asked and see if there is a Followers Prayer we might say together. That ended the conversation.

I didn't sleep that night. If I suggested a prayer to them, could it possibly be a prayer for the ages? If God's promises to me were true, then my followers will extend to the end of the age—far beyond my earthly life. What prayer would I want my followers to say together? I know from our Jewish prayers that there can be meaning in sharing the same prayer together, just as there is meaning in our individual prayers.

John the Baptizer was right. He had taught his disciples to fast and abstain and pray—and to remove themselves from the world. With my disciples, we prayed together every time we were together, always at the beginning and end of every day. But would there be a prayer my followers could say together?

The next day, I offered this prayer to them, which they cherished from that day on. It passed from one follower to the next:

O beloved Abba in heaven, holy is your name.
May your Kingdom come.
May your will be done on earth as it is in heaven.
May everyone have their daily bread to sustain them.
May we freely forgive others as we would want them to forgive us.
And save us during times of trial and temptation.
Rescue us from the clutches of evil and injustice.
May your kingdom come and your reign be forever.
Holy is your name, Lord. Amen.

Like a Child (Matthew 18:1—7)

One day my disciples approached me. I knew there had been some quarreling among them, some jousting for position. If they suspected one of them was getting closer to me, jealousy broke out. So their positions within my discipling community had become something of an issue. And I regretted that very much.

So, several disciples asked me, "Who is the greatest in the kingdom of heaven?" We were walking down the street of a village, and I knew that I needed something visual to help them see that all this jockeying for position was counter to God's way. Several children were playing nearby, and I asked a child to come over to me. I sat down on a large stone and invited the child to sit on my lap. And I told the disciples, "Truly I tell you, unless you allow yourselves to be transformed into a child, you will never enter the kingdom of heaven. You have to become humble, like this child, in order to be great in God's eyes. And when you welcome or encourage a child, like this young girl, you are welcoming me."

How did I know this? I knew this from my mother. She taught me this as a child. She told me, "You may be closer to the heart of God as a child than you will ever be the rest of your life. Because children are naturally open to life. They are eager to learn. They are non-judgmental. And they are humble—they don't build themselves up. You are like this right now, as a child, Jesus. You must remain this way throughout your life. Whatever else God will do through you, as God's vessel, you must be open; you must learn; you must not be judgmental; and you must remain humble."

Sound advice for me as a child. Sound advice for my disciples on this day. "Another thing," I said to them. "Never stand in the way of another person. They may be following God's way and you are the one unaware. Never be a stumbling block when someone is trying to find God in their lives. And never put your needs in front of theirs. If you can help them discover God more fully, help them walk down God's way, what better thing is there to do?"

Cursing a Fig Tree (Mark 11:12—14, 20—24)

My father loved figs. When they were in season, he was delirious! He loved them so much that he planted a fig tree in our side yard every year that one of his children was born. So, as the first-born, my fig tree was the oldest and largest. It was now producing figs in season and my father took delight in his "Jesus Tree." The James Tree was also growing, and so were all the other fig trees my father planted in honor of me or my siblings.

Because of this, I knew a lot about fig trees because I had watched that little grove of trees beside our house in Nazareth. It is impossible for a fig tree to bear bad fruit, for a tree is "known by its own fruit. Figs are not gathered from thorns, nor are grapes picked from a bramble bush." (Luke 6:44) Like all growing things, fig trees require a skilled and watchful eye, which my father provided. I once told a parable, thinking of my father. "A man planted a fig tree in his vineyard, and he kept coming back to it year after year looking for fruit, but after three years, the tree had produced no figs. He said to his vinedresser, "This tree is useless. Cut it down. Why should it be taking up space in my vineyard?" The vinedresser replied, "Sir, leave the tree one more season. I will dig around the tree and loosen the soil and turn manure into the soil. Then, it will bear fruit." (Luke 13:6—9)

I knew the meaning of the parable because I had watched my father and it usually took at least four years for his trees to produce figs. He said to us, "By the time your tree produces figs, you should also produce fruit in your life. You are then old enough to recognize all that God has done for you. When your figs mature, so must you!"

Knowing all of this, and the role that fig trees had played in my childhood family, it was all the more surprising when I expressed my anger one day at a lonely fig tree. At the time, I was feeling a lot of anxiety, because, contrary to advice from friends, I had triumphantly entered Jerusalem at Passover time. I came, even though I knew that the Chief Priests were prepared to arrest me and put an end to my ministry.

We had spent the night in Bethany, my village of safe refuge near Jerusalem. The disciples had enjoyed the wonderful hospitality of Mary and Martha and Lazarus. They had all begun the day in their home with a gracious and wonderful meal. I alone had fasted. I knew this day was going to be the most challenging of my life, and I thought it best to be spiritually prepared.

But no sooner had we left Bethany, than I began to feels pangs of hunger. My fasting had not fully prepared me for the challenges ahead, and I noticed a lonely fig tree up ahead. I raced toward it, ready to eat a freshly-picked fig. The tree was barren of fruit. Of course it was. Figs were not in season at this time of the year. This tree was full of leaves and the promise of fruit, but no fruit.

I was beside myself with anxious despair, and for some reason, I took it out on the fig tree. I cursed that tree. I said that day before my startled disciples, "May no one ever eat of the fruit of this tree!" My disciples heard it and were puzzled by the way I had cursed that tree.

The next morning, we were again walking from Bethany to Jerusalem and Peter said to me, "Rabbi, look! The fig tree that you cursed yesterday morning has withered." Indeed, the tree appeared to be dead. The life it had the day before was now gone.

I thought of my Jesus Tree in Nazareth, and of James' tree and the trees of my sisters and brothers, all planted with love by my father and cultivated by him. All were now producing a bounty of figs every year.

Then I turned to Peter and the others and said, "My faith has been shaken. I have already told you that the Son of Man will be handed over to the chief priests, and they will condemn him to death, and they will hand him over to the Gentiles, who will mock him, and spit upon him, and flog him, and then kill him, and after three days, he will rise again." (Mark 10:33—34)

"I need faith right now. I need to trust in God my Father. And you need faith as well. I also need your prayers. If we believe in the power of faith, we will prevail. God will prevail."

We never spoke of that cursed fig tree again. If I ever get back home to Nazareth, I'll plant a new fig tree in my father's memory.

What is it with all these Unclean Spirits? (John 10:24; Mark 5:7; Mark 3:11; Luke 4:31—36)

I'd have to say that most people didn't get it. I mean, they didn't really understand what I was all about. And that includes nearly all my disciples. We talked and talked but what they had in mind was far different than what I had in mind.

There was one group however that seemed to have me all figured out and it was the least likely of all. It was the unclean spirits that possessed some people. Through the people whom they possessed, they nearly always recognized my true identity and pronounced it dramatically.

What's the deal with that? Why would unclean spirits come closer than anyone else? And often they would reveal far more than I desired. I would often speak of my mission and role in the third person rather than speak plainly. The time wasn't yet right.

The unclean spirits loudly proclaimed, "You are the Son of God!" "What have you to do with me, Jesus, Son of the Most High God!" "I know who you are: the Holy One of God!"

I knew and I think God knew, that it was far too early for such pronouncements and I was careful not to make them. Perhaps part of it had to do with my being ready to say these things about myself and part of it had to do with others being able to hear it.

Sometimes, when others heard these pronouncements by unclean spirits, they perhaps considered the source and disregarded it. It was crazy talk. But each time I heard such statements, and it was with some frequency, the words jarred me into a new reality. I could not deny it: these were truthful statements. These were revealing statements. These spirits already understood. They already knew. They already were ready to proclaim.

Perhaps these unclean spirits knew the reality of my life before me. Could unclean spirits be used of God? Could they be God's way of saying to me: "This is who you are, Jesus"?

She Prepared Me for Death (Matthew 26:6—13)

I have some special friends who have stood with me through many trials and experiences. There's Lazarus, Mary and Martha, three siblings who lived in

Bethany, just outside Jerusalem. Whenever I was in the city of Zion, I stayed in their home and enjoyed their gracious hospitality. It was my home away from home. When I stayed with them, there were always "four of us," as poor Lazarus was usually out-numbered by his two sisters.

Because of all the time I spent there, I knew nearly all the residents of Bethany, including Simon a leper. He had been a friend of Mary, Martha and Lazarus for years. When he contracted the disease, the people of Bethany took special precautions so he could remain in his home instead of being sent off to a leper colony.

Simon wanted to invite me to his home. No righteous Jew would have ever entered his home because the leprosy was seen as a sign of his sinfulness. I knew it was no such thing. Simon was the same good man as before he contracted the disease and he had done nothing wrong to contract leprosy. It was his special challenge to face, and with strong perseverance, he was overcoming the disease—something very few people could do. And he never could have done it alone. The love of his entire village was involved.

So, Simon invited me to his home. As part of the precautions, Mary and Martha prepared everything in their home and brought it over to Simon's house. His skin lesions were healing now, but he wanted to take care and not spread his disease to me or any other guests.

I entered Simon's house. I've been around dozens of lepers, and I had no concern. My disciples didn't much want to follow me there, so I gave them the choice. Peter and Andrew and Judas came with me. When we entered, the role of hospitality belonged to Mary and Martha. They washed our feet and prepared the table. And the meal began with Martha mostly in charge of the food.

In the middle of the meal, Mary entered with an alabaster jar of very expensive ointment, and she poured it over my head as I sat at the table. This is a typical act of hospitality, except that this oil was much more expensive than usual. It was the kind of oil used to prepare a body for burial. Judas, the group treasurer, noticed the expensive nature of the ointment and he objected, "Why this waste? For this ointment could have been sold and given to the poor. Something less expensive could have been used as a simple act of hospitality." Mary backed away quickly, as Peter now joined in, "Why is she using a burial ointment? No one is dead here!"

I said to them, "Why do you trouble Mary? She has performed a wonderful service to me. By pouring this ointment on my body, she has prepared me for burial."

The disciples were taken back. Andrew said, "But you are not dead, Lord! And it's grotesque to pour burial oil over a living man. Are you eager for Jesus' death, Mary?" But Mary had far deeper spiritual insight than my disciples. She knew, far ahead of them, that when I returned to Jerusalem, my arrest and death were certain to follow. And she chose this night to prepare me spiritually for the challenging, awful days ahead. It was her way of saying to me: "This is going to get ugly. And you must be ready, Lord."

And my disciples were still in denial. Okay, maybe I was as well. Maybe my disciples reacted because I also was stunned for a few seconds, when Mary anointed me with burial oil. We use these oils to preserve and embalm deceased bodies.

But when I looked into this beautiful woman's face, my beloved friend, I knew what she was doing and why. And indeed, she had prepared me for facing what stood ahead. Without Mary, I might not have been ready. She was even ahead of me, spiritually, and certainly ahead of all the rest, in her prophetic vision of what was to transpire in Jerusalem. And rather than trying to talk me out of this crisis, she opted to prepare me for it.

I was deeply moved, even with fragrant burial ointment dripping from my hair. It was one of the most amazing experiences of my life. The ointment, Mary's prophetic vision, and my sudden recognition of what her symbolic actions meant.

My disciples nearly ruined it with their protests. I stopped them immediately, saying, "Truly, I tell you, wherever the gospel is proclaimed in the whole world, what Mary has done will be told in remembrance of her."

Not another word was said, as the sudden silence gave opportunity for those words to sink in. Mary blushed, but she didn't back down or back away—which wasn't her nature anyway.

Mary began to sing. A funeral dirge. A beautiful song of mourning:

> I lift my eyes to the mountains — from where will my help come?
> My help will come from the Lord, Maker of heaven and earth.
> He will not let your foot falter; your guardian does not slumber.
> Indeed, the Guardian of Israel neither slumbers nor sleeps.
> The Lord is your guardian; the Lord is your protective shade at
> your right hand.
> The sun will not harm you by day, nor the moon by night.
> The Lord will guard you from all evil; He will guard your soul.
> The Lord will guard your going and your coming from now and
> for all time. Psalm 130
> Amen.

The End Is Near (Mark 8:31—33; 9:30—32)

I gathered my disciples together. Time was drawing nigh. It wasn't my time on earth any more. It wasn't about my longevity any more. It was about God's time, the right moment for God. And I was integral to God's plan. Either I obeyed or I would have to go back on everything I stood for. And somehow I had to make my disciples understand. And that wasn't going to be easy because they wanted to keep things going.

"My beloved friends," I began. I was speaking to the women and men in my innermost circle. "I know you have learned from me, it's what disciples and rabbis do together. But, more than that, I need you to learn of me....no, more than that, I need you to learn me. I want you to take me into your heart, into your blood, into your bodies, into your minds, into your souls, into your dreams. Can you understand that? If you learn me, I know you will be ready for whatever comes next.

"You have seen with your eyes, more than you realize. You have heard with your ears, more than you can imagine. You understood more than you can put into words right now. All that God has spoken to me, I have spoken to you. I have planted God's Word within you. The vision that God has revealed to me, I have revealed to you. Cherish it. Hold onto it.

"I do not know what is coming. Our movement has been growing. People have been talking about us in the cities, in the countryside, in the villages, in the wilderness and the mountains. So much so that I have become a threat to our leaders in Jerusalem, the leaders of the Temple. They fear me now, because they see the signs I am performing, and they hear the words I teach, and the actions I take, and they fear if they wait longer, it will be too late. They think we could overwhelm them. That has never been my intent, but they do not know that.

"As a young boy, I remember talking with the scholars of our nation about the Anointed One. They asked me, 'Jesus of Nazareth, do you believe that God's Anointed One is coming?' And I answered them, 'God's Anointed One is already here. We have only to recognize him. He is at hand.'

"I am among you now. But not for long."

"'Why?,' they asked. 'Why must this be so? Can't we slow things down? Can't we get away, go back to the hills of Galilee? You know how much you enjoy your retreats in the mountains. Let's go there, right now, today, to pray, to seek God's will. How can this be God's will, to push the Temple leaders until they feel they have no choice? To disturb the peace so much that Rome will act? Let's leave now while we can, while there's time.'"

I listened. "But we cannot leave, because this is the Opportune Time. God is near! Learn me! Take me into your hearts and minds."

They looked at me as if I had beaten them with a stone. They were stunned, dazed. John asked, "Where is this leading?"

"I will tell you what has been revealed to me. I have had a vision from God. And God has told me that in a few days, I will be arrested. I will suffer greatly, even though I am innocent. I will be turned over to the Romans. They fear me, all of them, and now also the Romans. And you know what Romans do?"

Peter responded, "Please Jesus, no. Do not say these things. Let us leave. . .together. They will never find us in Galilee. Let us have some time alone."

"Peter, you are not listening to my words. You are just listening to your fears. I must be faithful to God's vision.

"Please know, all of you, that I have prayed that it be otherwise. I long to go back to Galilee with you, to have more time, to secure my place in the world. But God has revealed to me that there is no other way for me to rejoin Him except through terrible loss, awful suffering, innocent death.

Thomas said, "No Jesus, this cannot be." Mary Magdalene said, "We are not ready for this."

I looked intently at them, "You are ready. Trust me, you are, more than you realize. If I leave you, the burden of leadership falls upon you."

"But, listen to me, please, for there is another part of God's vision. And you need to hear this as well. Somehow, someway, death will be overcome. Not just mine, but death itself. Death will no longer have the final word. We never need to fear death again. I will die, surely, but I will also rise again, in your hearts and minds, as you learn me. I wish I could explain it more, but this is what I understand, all that God has given me. And it is enough.

"Now, I trust. And I need you to trust. I am ready. Are you?" A few nodded in agreement. Most of their heads hung low. "All that we have done together, all that we have revealed to the world about God's reign on earth, none of this will be wasted, not one word, not one miracle, not one act of compassion. It will speak through the ages.

"Listen, now, my friends. They are coming for me. Be strong. Be ready. Embrace God's vision for me, but also for you. You will face incredible sorrow. And you will receive incredible joy. Be strong now. Be ready. Let go and let God do something more wonderful still in your midst.

"Shhh. . . Listen. . . Goodbye, beloved friends."

A Supper to Prepare Them (Luke 9:46—49; Luke 14:7—11; Luke 22:7—23)

Perhaps to any outside observer, my disciples, the Twelve and the others, were not ready for my sudden departure. They were still immature in their understanding. None of them had any formal training, so what they learned, they learned from me. It wasn't but a few weeks ago when I came back among them, interrupting an argument they were having about which of them was the greatest! I could scarcely believe my ears. And, it wasn't all that long ago when James and John came to me with a ridiculous request, "Please, Master, let one of us sit at your heavenly kingdom on your right side and the other on your left." When the other disciples heard about this request, they were furious. These and other incidents convinced me that they weren't quite ready—even though events beyond my control convinced me that the time was near!

To the argument they were having about who was the greatest, Peter's family was visiting and I asked Peter's youngest child to join me in the center. Peter was one of the loudest of them all, arguing, with some merit, that he was the greatest. Peter's child stood in front of us, and I took him in my arms and said to them, "Whoever welcomes this child in my name, welcomes me, and whoever welcomes me welcomes the one who sent me." They still seemed in a fog. Then I concluded, "For the least among you is the greatest of all." (Luke 9:46—49)

"Let me tell you a story. When you are invited to a wedding banquet, should you walk in and sit at a place of honor around the table? Philip answered, "Well, I suppose if you are a guest of honor, then it's the right thing to do." I looked at Philip and said, "No, sit at the place furthest from the host. And then if the host sees you there, he will say to you, 'Come, my friend, move up beside me.' But if you take the honored place, then the host may have to ask you to move further down. Remember, all who exalt themselves will be humbled, and those who humble themselves will be exalted." (Luke 14:7—11)

We were making progress, but time was drawing nigh. We were in Jerusalem, and it was time for the Passover Meal, and I let it be known among my inner circle that I wanted to share this Passover Meal with them—they would be my guests. I arranged for the meal to be in the upper room of the home of John Mark's mother, where we often gathered in the city.

When they arrived, I tied a towel around my waist, kneeled before them, and began washing their feet, as a servant would do. They objected, but I said to them, "No, I have come to serve."

I wanted to have a kosher meal with them, but I also wanted them to never forget what might be our last supper together. For Jews, it is important to us to distinguish right from wrong, the pure from the defiled, good and evil. And the Torah is our guide to such matters.

It is not permissible to drink blood. Blood must be drained from or boiled out of meat and poultry. Only pious men trained in the law can prepare meat that is kosher. And every village, including Nazareth, had a butcher who was able to do this. It was a noble profession requiring someone of both skill and integrity.

I knew my disciples often responded best to the shock-value of a situation. Often, I would teach them by shocking them into responding in a new way. When Peter's son stood before us, obviously Peter was shocked to see his son treated as the guest of honor, instead of himself!

They thought we were just having another Passover Meal, but I knew it was our Last Supper and it was time for them to wake up. I said to them, "I have eagerly anticipated this Passover Meal together, for I tell you, we will not eat together again like this until God's purposes are fulfilled in my life."

Jews leave an untouched but filled chalice on the table. It is there for the Messiah, when he should join us at the Table. The remaining chalice is reserved for him and we dream of the day when we will drink of it together. It is a Cup of Anticipation.

At the end of the meal, I took the remaining chalice in my hands. I held it up. There were startled looks around the room. John started to object, but I motioned for silence. And I took a loaf of bread in my other hand, and held it up. I said to them, "This bread, represents my body. This cup, my blood. Tonight, I am holding these in my hands. But the day is coming soon when I will no longer be among you. But this bread, and this chalice, when you look to them, tonight and always, I want you to see me. More than that, when you drink of the chalice, and eat of the bread, I want you to take me into your bodies, into your souls, into your lives.

I was way out beyond kosher as I said, "Eat and drink of me, for I am God's sacrificial Lamb." And, miracle of miracles, something unexpected happened around the table. There was a sudden hush beyond any other we had shared together. All eyes were sober, filled with passion, as the bread and chalice were passed from one to another. Every eye followed them as they moved around the table.

"Once my physical presence is gone, you will still know me. As you eat of this bread and drink of this cup, I will always be among you and within you through God's Holy Spirit."

I sensed that this meal would prepare them for what stood ahead.

I've Never Died Before (Luke 23)

I've never died before. No one has. It's a once-in-a-lifetime experience. Not one person knows with certainty how they will die, or when. God knows.

And, therefore, we don't have practice at dying. I dreaded that. I was still very young, in my early 30's, and my public ministry had only lasted three years. Was that long enough to make a difference? Did I accomplish what was needed? Will my life be forgotten and my mission wasted? Is this God's plan?

Sure, I had those questions. In my case, I knew I faced great suffering and was certain to face a cruel death. Did I have the courage to endure this?

Incredibly, I did. When the final days came upon me, the mockery of trials, the flogging, the insults, I found a strength from within that I didn't know existed. I thought I would fall apart, cave in. But I learned that I had a greater strength within.

It was a strength in which I didn't feel a need to defend myself. I didn't try to get out of anything. Somehow, I was ready. And the more they flung at me, the more resolute I became. How did this happen? What was the source of this new-found strength? Once I was arrested, I literally had no fear. I was completely alone. My followers did not remain at my side, for the most part. And I, I had no fear.

Of course, I felt the physical pain, carrying the cross, the nails pounded into my flesh, my hands and feet. Excruciating pain. But I wasn't able to feel the spiritual pain, because I knew God was with me. Just once, I cried out, "My God, where are you?" But the words had no more than left my mouth that I knew the answer. "I am right here, Jesus, right beside you. Learn me, Jesus. Learn me, and trust when I tell you that death is no longer an ending. It is a beginning. Come to me, now, my beloved son." From the cross, it was those baptismal words I heard again. "My beloved."

From the cross, the women were there. I could look down and feel their pain. Their tears were so painful to watch. My own mother's tears! When the weight of my body pulled against the nails in my hands and feet, I could feel God's angels surround me, and lift me up, and the Voice of Heaven assured me, "Your life on earth may be finished. But you, Jesus, have just begun." In the midst of the pain and humiliation, I began to feel a strange sense of comfort.

And I can tell you, I died in comfort, hanging upon the cross. Strange? Perhaps. But the pain the Romans intended had no impact. Who could imagine? God had seen me through. Yes, my God had seen me through. I learned how great is our God!

And death? Why, death had lost its sting.

Chapter Two

Jesus as a Learner

Everyone Is a Learner

What if you were told that your newborn child could not learn? Would that not fundamentally alter every hope you have for your child? Your child could not learn to eat food, nor learn to walk or crawl, nor learn to form words, nor learn to copy the actions of others, nor learn to love or express love. "Your child cannot learn."

My two-month-old granddaughter had a dazed, "Where am I?" look on her face when she was first born. But now, she notices and is attracted to faces, to colors, to movement. You can see in her eyes that she can focus upon things around her. She is beginning to reach out and touch fascinating things with her hands. She is a learner.

We may have different capabilities, but every human being is a learner. If we weren't capable of learning, our lives would be radically diminished, fundamentally and downwardly re-defined. Human beings are always learning. Even those who experience a brain injury or have mental disabilities, can, for the most part, learn.

We may or may not learn healthy things. We may learn addictive behaviors. We may learn a devious way to take revenge on someone. We may learn self-loathing. And we may learn generosity and self-acceptance.

We learn—always—from exposure, from experience, from reflection, from making sense, from interaction, and from our mistakes. You and I can experience the same thing and you might learn a great deal, and I almost nothing. Some of us have huge appetites for learning and others less.

We can't learn everything or know everything. The world is far too complex for that. We each have natural propensities to learn certain things and stretch our base of knowledge in those directions. Advanced mathematical theory is not one of my natural interests. Therefore, I have learned little about it. We each have a strong appetite to learn those things that connect with our prior experiences. It is rare to learn something unless connections are first formed with what we already know. We don't learn out of "thin air."

What do you enjoy learning? Why?

We can learn by memorization. In Spanish or Arabic, we can learn to say, "How are you?" Yet we can also learn to problem solve, to think creatively, and to make meaning of life.

Learning is an internal activity. I can observe your attempt to learn as well as the outcome of your learning, but not the act of learning. At the end of the day, teachers ask, "Did my students learn anything today?" And the question can only be answered when students speak of what they learned. Tests are given in classrooms to determine what has been learned.

All animals learn. There are at least two kinds of learning: instinctual learning and acquired learning. When we were living in South Africa on a sabbatical, my wife, daughter and I were walking across downtown Johannesburg. Along the way, a group of eight young boys encircled us. One of them grabbed at my camera bag and I resisted. But then one of them kicked my young daughter to the ground, and something within me took over. I begin screaming at the top of my lungs to get attention, and I began kicking and punching like a wild animal. Instinct or self-preservation took over. When the boys finally ran off, I looked down at my wrist and discovered that one of them had cut me with something like a dull razor blade. It wasn't a deep cut, but I had reacted so violently that I hadn't even noticed sustaining that kind of injury. Such behavior isn't my style. I'm not a fighter. But when pressed into a corner, instinct took over.

Most animals have deep instinctual learning. The monarch butterflies begin in one area of Mexico and annually migrant north, nearly always following an identical path. Yet, those monarchs do not live to return to Mexico. That is the next generation. It's instinctual knowledge that "programs" them to know precisely what the previous generations knew.

My son and daughter-in-law have two pit bulls. My wife and I were traveling to Michigan and it would be the first time to meet their dogs. We had misgivings about their taking on that breed and more misgivings about sleeping in the same house with them. Our stereotypes couldn't have been more in error. These were large and muscular pit bulls, but they had no sense of their size and they loved to climb on the sofa and cuddle with whomever happened to be there! And if one cuddled, the other did as well. You haven't lived until you've had two large pit bulls sleeping on your lap!

Dogs will protect themselves. But they have to be taught to become fighting dogs. That's acquired learning. We human beings have instinctual learning. Sometimes, we just "know something" we weren't taught. Everyone has experienced this. But acquired learning requires teaching. And human beings excel at acquired learning.

There are at least two kinds of learning that arise from teaching: *Learning that Reinforces and Learning that Transforms.*

Both are essential. Reinforced learning is learning those things that strengthen and deepen what you already know. Most schooling, even in college, has to do with developing and reinforcing a body of knowledge. You keep adding to what you know.

Transformational learning is different. It is learning that re-arranges your assumptions, changes your perspective, re-orders your priorities, and shifts the foundation of your life. As a result of transformational learning, faith is typically in a very different place today compared to childhood.

If we engage exclusively in learning that only reinforces what we already know and in fiercely defending our understanding of life, then our learning becomes brittle. The boundaries of our world become more fixed. However, reinforced learning builds our base of knowledge, and helps us become logical and ordered in our thinking. Transformative learning makes us receptive to new perspectives. Our world enlarges.

We likely prefer to reinforce what we already know. It makes us comfortable and maintains life on a predictable plain. While reinforced learning tends to build upon what we already know, transforming learning opens our vision to new ways of seeing. Transformation is typically unsettling and frightening. It re-defines everything.

Spiritual conversion is transformative. The Holy Spirit may not slowly evolve us into the people God calls us to be. "The Christian faith by its very nature demands conversion. We cannot gradually educate persons through instruction in schools to be Christian."[1] God intervenes, interrupts, takes hold of us, and we are gripped by transformation. God is the instigator of transformative learning. The origin of reinforced learning is most often within ourselves. The origin of transformative learning comes from beyond.

Because most spiritual learning is transformational, it means that our approach to learning in church must be very different. It's not so much a

---

1. Westerhoff, *Will Our Children Have Faith?*, 38.

matter of memorizing or adding to what we already know. It is opening ourselves to what the Spirit introduces. It is most often unexpected learning.

We tend to remember transformative learning. My family spent a sabbatical living with pastors and their families in the black townships and homelands of South Africa during the waning days of apartheid. We were invited to live with Desmond and Beverley Hoffmeister in the coloured township of Ennerdale. Almost immediately, we began talking into the early morning hours on a nightly basis. Their world of inequality and racial injustice was something we knew only second-hand. And our world of equality for women and sexual minorities was new to them. And those transformational conversations stretched all four of us to the point that we would never again be the same. I remember well the people, the time, the place, the conversations.

Jesus spoke often of our need to "be born anew." (John 3:3–7) He also taught, "Unless you change and become like little children, you will never enter the kingdom of Heaven." (Matt 18:3) And the opening word of his public ministry was, "Repent." (Mark 1:15) Turn around. And Paul wrote that "If anyone is in Christ, there is a new creation; everything old has passed away." (2 Cor 5:17) This is transformational learning. And the Bible is filled with it. (Isa 43:19)

Human Becomings

To be sure, human beings are *human becomings*. We enter this world with so much to learn, completely dependent upon our providers and teachers. We must learn to speak a language, learn to crawl and walk, and learn to interact with an ever-widening world. It's true of all human babies. And learning is the "engine" that drives our becoming.

Albert Einstein surely showed early signs of incredible intelligence. Mozart was a child prodigy, writing music before the age of six. But that does not mean that Einstein or Mozart weren't capable of learning. Actually, the opposite is true: they were incredible, eager learners throughout life.

Our becoming is our most compelling human attribute. It reflects growth, discernment, and re-definition that call us to our highest and best. On the other hand, fear and intimidation thwart the human spirit and learning.

Do you see yourself as a Human Becoming?

Rev. Galusha Anderson, a Civil War era pastor in St. Louis, told the story of one of his young leaders making an appointment soon after Pastor Anderson began to speak out against slavery and the Confederacy. This young leader was from the South and desired an open conversation to understand why his pastor would take such a controversial stand and make many members of his church uncomfortable. They talked quite a while and apparently Rev. Anderson made some head-way with the young man. After their talk, the young man "began to think as never before. He now observed that all the newspapers and journals that came to his house were pro-slavery and secession; and he decided to secure for daily reading some that presented the opposite view. He at once subscribed to two Union papers. He looked over his library and did not find a book in it that was antagonistic to slavery. He went at once to a bookstore and bought three anti-slavery books, which he carefully read. Within a few days his mind was completely revolutionized. He had decided what to do. . . He soon called (his pastor) and said: 'Pastor, you made one serious mistake. You ought to have preached against succession at least three months before you did.'" His change of mind and allegiance cost the young man dearly. "It broke up old associations, and for a time at least made lifelong friends enemies."[2]

This describes one young man's "becoming." It is an example of transformative learning in which the very foundations of his life began to shake and crumble. The same thing happened to me during my first year in seminary. In attending the seminary of my choice, I thought I was expressing my open-mindedness. But I was woefully unprepared for the critical study of scripture. What I was learning in the classroom shook my world. My faith began to wobble. I could not easily justify what I had thought to be true with what I was learning to be true. And then I painfully re-built my faith, based upon a profoundly different world-view that changed the course of my life from that moment on.

Even President Abraham Lincoln was a "becomer" in terms of his understanding of race relations and slavery. He was born in a slave state of Kentucky and married the daughter of a slave-owner. Even though he personally abhorred slavery, early in his career, he found ways to accommodate slavery in the Southern states. For a time he supported freeing African Americans and then sending them back to Africa. Even during his presidency, he continued to refine his views, eventually believing that the Civil War was justified to abolish slavery once and for all from the entire nation, including the Southern states. One meeting that had an impact on Lincoln occurred on August 10, 1863. It was in the White House between Lincoln and Frederick Douglass. At that time, anyone could walk into the White House and ask for an appointment with the President. Douglass did exactly that. He walked in off the street, asked for an appointment and sat

2. Anderson, *A Border City During the Civil War*, 149.

down amidst all the white people waiting to see Lincoln. Within minutes, Douglass walked ahead of the others as Lincoln was eager to meet him. They met and conversed as equals, a conversation and ongoing relationship that had a profound impact on both men. Lincoln was evolving his thoughts on slavery throughout his life.

We are human *becomings,* even the greatest among us.

Robbed of our potential to learn, we would merely repeat the tried, unable to change, lacking the power to create, like puppets on a string. It is the capacity to learn that allows us to be creators, artists, poets, authors, designers, inventors, discoverers, explorers, solvers, repairers, or change agents.

Insight and Inspiration

Learning often accompanies a new insight. Insight is "sight" from within, inner vision, inner illumination. As a word, "insight" dates back to the year 1200, *"innsihht,"* meaning, "sight with the eyes of the mind."

Inspiration, complementarily, most often "comes to us" rather than produced by us. We are "inspired" and therefore gain new insights about our lives. Inspire, literally, means to "breathe into." And most often, from ancient times, it carried the connotation of divine intervention. God "breathing into," inspiring us. Poets, artists, and musicians know this. Columnist David Brooks wrote recently about inspiration: Moments of inspiration "feel transcendent, uncontrollable and irresistible. . . The person in the grip of inspiration has received, as if by magic, some new perception, some holistic understanding, along with the feeling that she is capable of more than she thought. . . Inspiration is not earned. . ., but is a gift that goes beyond anything you could have deserved."[3]

I was at a peace conference and I heard one speaker talk of Jesus as a teacher of peace. I drove home from McMinnville, Oregon to Seattle with that on my mind. Was this really true, or did this point merely serve the speaker's agenda? And the inspiration came to me that Jesus indeed was a peace teacher and his primary message centered around the Hebrew idea of shalom. Anxious not to lose those thoughts, I pulled my car off the road no less than seven times as insights kept coming to me. This resulted in my writing a book, *PeaceTeacher, Jesus' Way of Shalom.* Prior to that trip home, I had not explored these ideas. Inspiration sent me in an entirely new direction. Insights followed.

Human beings are wired for insight, inspiration, and learning. It is part of our DNA. With these special gifts, it is obvious that God isn't finished with

3. Brooks, *New York Times Op-Ed,* A27.

us yet. God keeps speaking — maybe not audibly, but from within. Without insight, inspiration, and learning, we would have no way to hear God or co-create with God. God continuously introduces us to "all things new" (2 Cor 5:17; Isa 65:17). Jesus' central message was that God is on the cusp of introducing a new world, a new Reign, a new way of becoming. (Mark 1:15)

Made in God's image, we are restless for more; for More! We cannot be satisfied with things as they are. And this dissatisfaction, restlessness, and yearning compel us to be learners. As learners, we best reflect God. God is never satisfied with things as they are. "For the creation waits with eager longing. . . We know that the whole creation has been groaning in labor pains until now. . ." (Rom 8:19, 22) "This is the Lord's doing; it is marvelous in our eyes." (Ps 118:23; 2 Cor 5:18a) We become a part of God's new creation through learning and receptivity.

A frequent theme of Apostle Paul was encouragement to learn, grow, and mature in Christ. He spoke of wanting "to know Christ and the power of his resurrection and the sharing of his sufferings" (Phil 3:10). But then he writes, "Not that I have already obtained this or have already reached the goal; but I press on to make it my own, because Christ Jesus has made me his own. . . (F)orgetting what lies behind and straining forward to what lies ahead, I press on toward the goal for the prize of the heavenly call of God in Christ Jesus." (Phil 3:10–14)

Interpreting Life

Life requires interpretation. Otherwise, it is an utter puzzle. Life doesn't come ready-made. We have to make sense of it. We have to discover ways to put life together. And in every human journey there comes an early point in life when we realize that our life will be what we make of it. We are born with restlessness, with yearning, and a deep desire to "make something" of our lives. The resolution of this yearning will not be resolved for us. We each have to make sense of our own lives. Human beings are meaning-making beings. Thus, life requires interpretation. How tragic it is to watch someone avoid making sense of their lives.

Life isn't lived backwards, but rather forward. Yet, a backward perspective is invaluable to interpretation of our lives. We gain wisdom by looking back over our lives. We are struck by how all the loose ends fit together. We are struck with the question: Was the timing of this coincidental? Was it Spirit-led? We make meaning out of our lives by looking back. Henri Nouwen wrote, "We first look backward to see how our lives' seemingly unrelated events have brought us to where we are. . . Forgetting the past is like turning our most intimate teacher against us. It is the guarantee that we cannot find the way to trust and hope."[4]

Yet, *"now"* is where life is lived. And we must never remove our gaze from the road ahead less nostalgia overtakes us. Frederick Buechner writes, "What quickens my pulse now is the stretch ahead rather than the one behind, and it is mainly for some clue to where I am going that I search through where I have been, for some hint as to who I am becoming or failing to become that I delve into what used to be. . . (E)ven then God was addressing me out of my life as he addresses us all."[5]

In the present-tense, we have much to figure out as we go. Learning is essential as we stand at the crossroads of our lives. This can be called intellectual humility, the awareness that we always have more to learn. There is also intellectual arrogance, my wanting others to be impressed with how much I have learned! Jesus advocated intellectual humility. He said in a prayer, "I thank you, Lord of heaven and earth, because you have hidden these things from the wise and the intelligent and have revealed them to infants; yes, Father, such was your gracious will." (Luke 10:21) Jesus is offering a prayer of praise to God upon the return of seventy of his followers after going into villages and towns proclaiming, "The kingdom of God has come near to you." (Luke 10:9b) Jesus is attacking intellectual snobbery, and praising those willing to be open to learn what the Spirit reveals.

Is it possible to stop interpreting life, which is the same thing as no longer learning? I once served as a pastor to a person who seemed to have stopped interpreting life. Every value and every belief she held seemed to come from her mother, who was a very strong and opinionated matriarch. Though long dead, she continued to wield a huge influence over her daughter to the point that her daughter's value and belief system seemed stuck in time—as much as 70 years before. Occasionally, I would try to get her to see a situation in a different way, but there was no budging her. She knew the truth and was confident that her perspective on reality was the only acceptable one. No other alternative could be considered. She quoted her mother as if she was sitting in the next room. If the world had changed in the decades since her mother's passing, nothing had changed in this daughter's perspective.

When we aren't open to learning new insights, then our lives take on the appearance of being frozen in time. We no longer learn or unlearn. And the people around us pay a price for our intransigence.

4. Nouwen, *Turn My Mourning into Dancing,* 59.
5. Buechner, *The Sacred Journey,* 6.

Faith vs. Certainty

I grew up in a faith environment in which the goal was to be as certain of one's faith as possible. We believed in an unchanging God and a rock-solid gospel. We sang the song,

> *On Christ the solid rock I stand, all other ground is sinking sand.*
> The second stanza states,
> *When darkness seems to hide His face,*
> *I rest on His unchanging grace;*
> *In every high and stormy gale,*
> *My anchor holds within the vale.*[6]

Doesn't it make sense that the stronger your faith, the more certain you are of what is true and trustworthy?

Yet, my faith journey since childhood has led me to question the consequential relation between faith and certainty. We assume Jesus advocated rock-solid faith when he told the well-known story of the house built on rock or on sand. But is that really the point of his parable?

"Everyone then *who hears these words of mine and acts on them* will be like a wise man who built his house on rock. The rain fell, the floods came, and the winds blew and beat on that house, but it did not fall, because it had been founded on rock. And everyone *who hears these words of mine and does not act on them* will be like a foolish man who built his house on sand. The rain fell, and the floods came and the winds blew and beat against the house, and it fell—and great was its fall." (Mt 7:24—27)

We assume this parable teaches that our faith needs to be rock-solid. But rather, isn't the point of this parable to describe what happens when we disconnect beliefs from actions? Or what happens when our faith is not expressed by our actions? Or what happens when faith is kept private and not expressed publicly? Or what happens when we are hypocritical (a term Jesus used 16 times in the Gospel of Matthew)? The parable doesn't describe faith itself as a solid rock; rather, faith expressed in one's actions is solid like a rock. And those who mouth words of faith, but whose actions are inconsistent with those words, are building their faith on sand. In other words, faith is stronger when actions and faith are in sync.

A few years ago, I was going through my father's file cabinet in the basement of our family home. My mother had just died and we were emptying the house. In the back of one folder, I found a journal that my father had written when he was in his twenties. In it he spoke of a nagging doubt about whether God was truly involved in his life. My father questioned whether

6. lyrics by Edward Mote, 1834.

God had a design on his life and how he would discern it. I was stunned to read this journal because he had never spoken with me about this nagging doubt which seemed to stay with him through his twenties.

I wish he had shared that with me because I encountered all kinds of doubts and questions in my teen and young adult years and it would have been very encouraging to have known of my father's earlier struggle.

But doubt wasn't encouraged in the church to which we belonged. Nor were questions. Being strong, definite and certain were valued. Whenever doubt entered one's mind, it was important to get rid of it as quickly as possible. Doubts were the Devil's playground. It was a healthy and wonderful church in many ways, but I wish I had been taught to value questions.

In my childhood church, by my junior high years, I was growing restless with Sunday School. It wasn't appropriate to raise honest questions and I had lots of questions. I was looking forward to the older high school Sunday School class. It was taught by a man who later taught me how to approach life's deepest mysteries. He ignored the denominational curriculum and instead based his hour with the teenagers asking questions and honoring their questions. And his classroom was packed on Sunday mornings, not only with youth from our church but from churches across town.

At the beginning of the summer before I was to graduate into this Senior High Class, one of the deacons complained about the teacher, saying that he was sowing seeds of doubt within the young people. The deacons dismissed the teacher. By the fall when I entered the class, it was taught by a kindly man who read the quarterly to us in a monotone voice, and by the end of the fall, there were only 4 students left.

In my upbringing, we prized certainty. Yet since childhood, I have experienced doubt, not as the enemy of faith, but as a partner to faith. Doubt carries the potential to truly deepen faith. Questions open the door to new insights.

Richard Rohr writes, ". . .Jesus' questions are to reposition you, make you own your unconscious biases, break you out of your dualistic mind, challenge your image of God or of the world, or present new creative possibilities. He himself does not usually wait for or expect specific answers. He hopes to call forth an answering person . . . Jesus asks questions, good questions, unnerving questions, realigning questions, transforming questions. He leads us into liminal and therefore transformative space, much more than taking us into any moral high ground of immediate certitude or ego superiority. . . He leaves us betwixt and between, where God and grace can get at us, and where we are not at all in control."[7]

7. Dear, *The Questions of Jesus*, xxii, xxiii.

Since Jesus used questions so effectively throughout his ministry with his followers and the crowds, why would we assume his questions have fallen silent on his followers today? Why would we assume that today Jesus raises only certainties and not questions? The Greek word, *erotao*, means to ask a question and is used 49 times in the Gospels. Another Greek word, *eperotao*, meaning "to ask," is used 52 times. In the Gospel of Luke, Jesus asked 89 teaching questions. In Matthew, 85, and in Mark, 47 questions.

Jesus did not teach certitude, but rather taught in paradox and irony. He rarely explained the paradoxes he told. His use of paradox was meant to dislodge people from their certitude. Jesus seemed perfectly comfortable leaving his "students" puzzled without a certain answer. Even his disciples were frequently left scratching their heads, trying to figure Jesus out. He didn't offer a great deal of help. As Rohr stated above, Jesus hoped "to call forth an answering person." Seeking and refining our answers is a life-long journey.

Here is a sampling of Jesus' many paradoxes:

- Perhaps his greatest teaching, the Beatitudes (Matt 5:3–12) is a collection of nine paradoxes, statements that do not appear to be true but in fact are.

- He said, ". . .among those born of women no one has arisen greater than John the Baptist, yet the least in the kingdom of heaven is greater than he." (Matt 11:11)

- "Whoever becomes humble like this child is the greatest in the kingdom of God." (Matt 18:4)

- ". . .whoever wishes to be great among you must be your servant, and whoever wishes to be first among you must be your slave, just as the Son of Man came not to be served, but to serve. . ." (Matt 20:26b-28a; Mark 10:43–44)

- "For those who want to save their life will lose it, and those who lose their life for my sake, and for the sake of the gospel, will save it. For what will it profit them to gain the whole world and forfeit their life?" (Mark 8:35–36; Luke 9:24–25)

- "Whoever wants to be first must be last of all and servant of all." (Mark 9:35c)

- "It is easier for a camel to go through the eye of a needle than for someone who is rich to enter the kingdom of God." (Mark 10:25)

- "But many who are first will be last and the last will be first." (Mark 10:31)

- "I thank you, Father, Lord of heaven and earth, because you have hidden these things from the wise and the intelligent and have revealed them to infants. . ." (Luke 10:23bc)

- "For all who exalt themselves will be humbled, and those who humble themselves will be exalted." (Luke 14:11; 18:14b)

- The wedding banquet parables told by Jesus are paradoxical, as frankly, are nearly all Jesus' parables.

Clearly, Jesus used paradox, parable and questions as his primary teaching tools. And all these approaches were intended to get people thinking, questioning, and searching.

So, what is faith, anyway? We have this naïve idea that the opposite of faith is doubt. Yet, how can that be when periods of doubt often lead to deeper faith? How can that be when we follow a question and arrive at more profound faith?

The opposite of faith is not doubt, but certainty! The author of Hebrews writes, "Now faith is the assurance of things hoped for, the conviction of things not seen." (11:1) If I am absolutely convinced of something beyond a shadow of a doubt, little faith is required to trust it. I believe that Tuesday follows Monday. I have little doubt about it, and therefore it doesn't require much faith from me.

I am convinced that my employer will pay me twice a month. That doesn't require much faith to believe because I only need to look at my checking account to notice automatic deposits every two weeks.

However, some questions require more faith: Will my employer choose to keep employing me? Will my employer continue to have the funds to pay me? Am I doing work that satisfies me beyond the paycheck? Does my work matter to anyone? Is my work worthwhile?

Faith is necessary when we believe what cannot be proven, what isn't obvious, what can't be seen. When confronting life's mysteries, we rely on faith. Faith arises, not from certainty, but from mystery, from life's hiddenness. Faith is necessary because of life's darkness, not from the bright light of day. Faith shines light in the darkness. Faith offers a way to navigate the darkness.

Apostle Paul wrote at the end of his great love chapter, "For we know only in part, and we prophesy only in part, but when the complete comes, the partial will come to an end. . . For now we see in a mirror, dimly, but then we will see face to face. Now I know only in part, then I will know fully, even as I have been fully known." (I Cor 13:9–10, 12) For now "we know only in part," thus, we have faith that someday the whole picture will be revealed.

The reason that faith is so profound is that nearly anything of signifi-cance in life cannot be proven and isn't obvious. Darkness would overwhelm us without faith.

I believe in love. I have faith in the power of love. But love can't be proven and it can't be seen. I believe in hope, even though the circumstances of life don't often support that belief. I believe that God will ultimately pre-vail, and again, the circumstances don't often support that. I believe that our world was created with a lot of goodness in it. Again, that can't be proven. These convictions require faith, sometimes a great deal of faith. The truth is that the most significant things in life can't be proven and involve some degree of mystery. Throughout our earthly journey, we know "only in part."

Science is based on theories and hypotheses and these must be con-stantly challenged by questions and doubts so that they hold to be true over time. Is there is such a thing as scientific certainty? A friend had to take one last course in the sciences so he signed up for advanced mathematical theory. It sounded easy to him. On the first day, the professor said, "I'm going to tell you my assignment for the final exam so you can reflect on it all semester long. I will ask you to write a forty-page paper on why $1 + 1 = 2$." After my friend became aware of all the nuances of that 'simple formula,' it was one of the toughest assignments of his college years.

The opposite of faith isn't doubt. Doubt is one of the engines that drives faith into deeper, more profound places. The opposite of faith is certainty because certainty freezes faith in its tracks. The more certain I am of God, the more rigid my beliefs become.

Are you afraid to experience doubt?

Faith and doubt are like two voices in a duet. One enriches and comple-ments the other. Faith may very well be the melody and doubt the harmony. Both are indispensable in a duet. You can have faith without doubt, but it is doubt that adds the depth, meaning and relevancy to faith. How can we repent and keep turning to God without questioning where we have been? Thus, without questioning, there can be no *metanoia*, no turning toward God. Certainty kills the beauty of the song.

Professor Renita Weems writes, "The truly remarkable transformation is not the one from unbelief to belief nor from despair to hope. The truly re-markable (and frightening) transformation is from dogma to wonder, from belief to awe."[8] It is the transformation from certainty to mystery.

I am drawn to the father of the young epileptic boy in the Gospel of Mark who brought his son to Jesus. The father stated to Jesus, "If you can

8. Weems, *Listening for God, a Minister's Journey through Science and Doubt*, 187.

heal him. . ." Jesus took exception to the man's lack of faith. Finally, the loving father said, "I believe, help my unbelief." And only then Jesus healed the boy of seizures. The father was not placing belief and unbelief as polar opposites but rather in creative tension with each other. He was suggesting they belong together as in a duet. He was on a journey of expanding faith. He wasn't there yet, but this was the new thrust of his life. (Mark 9:23—25)

In 1986, I was driving my family with our two young children across the state of Tennessee. I rounded a corner and ran into the rear of a slow-moving dump truck. My wife, in the back seat in a seat belt, experienced a counter-coup concussion resulting in a brain injury. Our children, thankfully, were not seriously injured.

During the months and years of my wife's recovery, I experienced challenges of faith with many swirling doubts. I was fairly confident that it was an accident I could have avoided. I made a driving error for which my wife paid the price. And her long rehabilitation and journey of self-acceptance was open-ended. Neither of us could say, "Now, it is behind us." I experienced many self-doubts. Where was God in the midst of this calamity? How can God see us through? Will our marriage survive? How will our children be affected by this crisis?

Even in that crisis, I never stopped believing in God. In fact, members of my congregation stated that I preached my way out of it. I think, for the most part, they were understanding and supportive. But along the way, I easily could pray, "I believe, help my unbelief." For several years, belief and unbelief were actively in creative tension in my life as well as for my wife. Fortunately, we were able to voice these new questions thrust upon us by this accident. It was the questions that guided us through.

I would give anything to have that day over again. . .to not make the same mistake. But experiencing God in that darkest of nights brought my faith to a new place where an untested faith could never be. If I had believed that faith was the opposite of doubt, I would have lost my faith. Throughout that season, I never believed that God was failing me because I had so many doubts, questions and uncertainties. It was doubts and questions that became my guide through the toughest years of this crisis.

If faith is certainty. . .

. . .then the foundation of my faith is concretized in rigid, unchanging thinking.

. . .then my task is to defend and protect my faith at all costs.

. . .then I devote my life reinforcing what I already believe.

. . .then I have already arrived at my "promised land," and I can freeze my beliefs where they are and wait for eternal life "as is."

. . .then I shun questions and close up cracks caused by doubt.

. . .then my beliefs cannot be challenged or questioned.

. . .then I spend the rest of my life trying to convince others of my beliefs and truths. I'm certain that what works for me, works for everyone. My answers are the most important reality.

. . .then my faith approaches idolatry as I become satisfied with my definitions, my assumptions, my truths.

. . .then I avoid or explain away paradox, mystery, absurdity or contradiction.

. . .then I must defend what I know and resist learning anything new or contradictory.

But if faith and doubt are in creative tension, everything changes, introducing a different world-view. If faith arises from questions and doubts. . .

. . .then I'm respectful of what I don't know and what I still haven't figured out.

. . .then I'm less troubled by ambiguity, by paradox, and by life's mysteries and absurdities.

. . .then my faith is a work in progress, not a completed act.

. . .then I become convinced that "God is still speaking," and that God can interrupt or intervene in my life.

. . .then I avoid rigid boundaries around my faith and become less judgmental.

. . .then my faith isn't defensive in posture; I listen to a multitude of voices which I find exhilarating. God speaks to me in surprising ways and from unexpected sources.

. . .then I'm happy to share my truth as I see it now without becoming confused that I have arrived at The Truth.

. . .then I can be comforted by my faith as it continues to unfold, and confident that "God isn't finished with me yet."

. . .then I am less likely to have a debilitating crisis of faith and more likely to listen, to respond, and discern my way through any challenge life places before me.

. . .then I am an engaged learner.

Peter Berger, sociologist of religion, said, "The basic fault lines today are not between people with different beliefs but between people who hold these beliefs with an element of uncertainty and people who hold these beliefs with a pretense of certitude. . . There is a middle ground between fanaticism and relativism."[9]

Is your faith built on certainty?

A faith built on certainty tends toward fanaticism and fundamentalism. Fundamentalists are convinced that they alone possess the only version of the truth. They are unmoved by any evidence to the contrary. The word certain, comes from the Latin word, *certus,* which means "fixed or settled."

Faith vs. Certitude

Faith is open to what it doesn't yet know, what it hasn't yet explored, and the question it hasn't yet asked. Faith is open to on-going revelation. Faith is open to God's Intervening Spirit. It is not complacent or self-satisfied. Faith will not stand still. It is active and engaged. Faith can be a dynamic force in our becoming. It must be growing or it becomes stale, even dead.

I was speaking recently with a young adult in my congregation who is actively engaged in a spiritual quest. She has many questions, an inner restlessness that causes her to keep reading, meditating, and searching. And her search has led her into many wonderful discoveries and into a more profound relationship with God. She told me that her image of God as a child was of a Heavenly Father who was far off, keeping a ledger of judgement on each of us as to the right and wrong things we do. Yet, because of her restlessness, she had more recently discovered God in "centering prayer," a God near to her, accompanying her along life's journey, and helping her to face the crossroads of her life. No one else in her immediate family possesses her spiritual restlessness or her hunger for God, at least in obvious ways. I helped her see that this was a special gift she had received, not something to regret. Her restlessness has led her to a much more profound relationship with God revealed in Christ.

Certitude, on the other hand, is a religious system that knows it all, has already "arrived," and isn't open to honest questions. To those enveloped by certainty, God has already revealed all truth, fully and clearly. God has already spoken all that needs to be said. Certitude is Rock-Solid, and therein lies its weakness. Certitude will eventually get stuck, unable to adapt

9. Berger, *Christian Century*, 1997.

to changing circumstances. Noted Christian ethicist and theologian David P. Gushee wrote: "I have spent much of my adult life trying to help young people make the transition from brittle certainties to a more supple and mature faith that usually (but not always) leaves them stronger for having wrestled with the tough questions."[10]

Peter Enns states, ". . .doubt is not the enemy of faith, a solely destructive force that rips us away from God, a dark cloud that blocks the bright warm sun of faith. Doubt is only the enemy of faith when we equate faith with certainty in our thinking."[11] And again Enns states, "Doubt is sacred. Doubt is God's instrument, will arrive in God's time, and will come from unexpected places—places out of your control. And when it does, resist the fight-or-flight impulse. Pass through it—patiently, honestly, and courageously for however long it takes. True transformation takes time."[12]

Are Doubts Enough?

But are questions and doubts enough? Is it enough to go through life following our questions, but never embracing answers? Is it enough to doubt—only to doubt? I've met a number of people like this, who begin and end with questions or doubts and never get beyond it. Each one of them seemed thoroughly stuck.

Perhaps we should follow the example of the father who met Jesus and prayed, "I believe; help my unbelief!" Questions and doubts alone do not satisfy. They are not enough.

There needs to be a creative or dynamic tension between our faith—our relationship with God—and the mystery that is inherent in a divine-human relationship. There needs to be a dynamic tension between our heart-felt faith—and the questions that cause faith to deepen.

I noted above that faith and doubt are like singing a duet—the duet cannot happen without both voices. If we become satisfied with our doubts, then we are frightened to learn anything new. Learning requires that we reach some observations and draw tentative conclusions. If we swim in a sea of questions, we learn nothing.

Learning is decisional! Suppose you and I work in the same company. And the company experiences a serious, unexpected upheaval and

10. Gushee, *Still Christian, Following Jesus Out of American Evangelicalism*, 24–25.

11. Enns, *The Sin of Certainty, Why God Desires Our Trust More Than Our 'Correct' Beliefs*, 157.

12. Enns, *The Sin of Certainty, Why God Desires our Trust More Than Our 'Correct' Beliefs*, 164.

disruption. We can each learn different things from this uncomfortable experience. I can learn that I will never again work for others. You can learn that if you had only changed one or two behaviors, you could have been instrumental in helping that company reach better outcomes. We were in the very same situation and we made different decisions about what we learned from this caustic experience. We make decisions all the time, small and profound, which effect what we learn and the conclusions we make.

We live with our faith day by day in authentic ways. However, life stretches faith—challenges faith—pushes against faith. It always does. Our child gets sick. Our spouse threatens to leave. Our best friend gets cancer. Our son is fired from his job due to a moral lapse. We break from our best friend because of a political disagreement.

And our faith, that once held us together, no longer can. And questions arise—natural, healthy questions—not made-up or imposed questions. And we can either deny the questions, avoid the questions, or follow them.

By following them, our faith enters a crisis. But, nearly always, it comes out on the other side, with a deeper understanding and appreciation of the Spirit's role in our lives. Our spouse threatens to leave—but one night, we have an entirely different kind of conversation—about hope—about second starts—about not giving up—and suddenly we find ourselves in a new place with God leading us together in a way we could never have anticipated.

My best friend has cancer. And I depend upon this best friend as an indispensable anchor in my life. He's dying and all our prayers for God to cure him are for naught. But instead of curing my friend, at the end, we finally take our friendship to an entirely new level. A depth emerges between us we could only imagine. Joking and sarcasm are now replaced with confessional conversations. My friend dies, but in dying he has left me with an incredible faith in the worthiness of life, and the trustworthiness of eternal life.

My son makes a terrible mistake at work. Instead of trying to fix his problem, I decide he must work his way through it—but with me, his father, at his side in a non-judgmental way. And through this experience, I learn something incredible—that our God is a God of fresh beginnings and new chapters. My son learns an invaluable lesson, and I learn how to be his adult friend.

My parents, relatively young and vital, are driving home from a visit with my family and are involved in a fatal accident. Suddenly, they are gone and their loss sends me into a tail-spin. I am totally unprepared for their deaths. And I enter into a very dark season. However, after a few months, I find myself sitting on the back steps of our porch, and I'm having a conversation with my dad as if he was really there. And while I feel a deep sense of satisfaction, I wonder if I'm going crazy. But then I talk to others and several say, "Sure, I have conversations with my (deceased) parents all the time. It's deeply meaningful." So, I decide to have a conversation with my mother about a problem I'm having with my daughter. And she says exactly what I needed to hear. My parents are an active part of my collective memory and consciousness and I learn, with deep gratitude, that I carry them with me to the end of my life.

All of these experiences can be so devastating as to make us lose our faith, or turn away from God. But, by introducing questions and doubts along our faith journey, we find ourselves on a higher plain than we could ever have imagined. Our faith deepens and matures.

The father in scripture was losing his beloved son. He was in real crisis. He surely prayed, "Let me die, but save my son!" He asked God, "How can you let this happen to my son instead of me?" Then he prayed, "What can I do?" He had heard about Jesus. And by asking around, he found that Jesus was in his area of Galilee and he sought him out. He came to Jesus with all his questions and doubts, yet also with an openness of faith—and Jesus eventually embraced the man, embraced his faith, and embraced his confession. It wasn't only the son who was healed that day. It was the father who was also healed—as he discovered that God does start-overs—for his son and also for the father.

Questions and doubts on their own can be a way to avoid God, and avoid maturation in God's ways. But this duet of life, faith and doubt, opens new horizons.

What if we made "faith" and "doubt" into verbs, into actions or engagements? So, they would become "faithing" and "doubting." Faith is something you have. Faithing is something in which you engage. Doubt is also something you have. Doubting is something you engage in.

If you engage in faithing and doubting, perhaps not all the time, but at those moments that call for it, this double engagement adds rich possibilities. It even offers a way out of a locked room with no doors. Back to the duet analogy, they each add unique voices. If faith is something you have, then it's something you can lose, or something that can fall apart. But if faithing is something in which you engage, then it's something in which you are involved throughout life's journey. And when our engagement in faithing is pressed or challenged, as it often is, doubting is an engagement that adds the elasticity, flexibility and creativity necessary to find a way through. If you find yourself in a no-exit room, doubting locates a door. Engagements in faithing and doubting, therefore, are not competitive or adversarial, but complementary and necessary.

What about uncertainty? An agnostic is often deeply committed to uncertainty, and committed to not reaching conclusions. Uncertainty isn't a permanent address. It isn't a place to stay. But often as we deal with life's difficult situations, we have to live with uncertainty for a time. But committing ourselves to remain uncertain isn't likely much better than committing ourselves to certitude. Neither require much faith.

Confidence vs. Certitude

Honest faith builds spiritual confidence. Confidence isn't rigid, but it does imply delight with where a spiritual journey is headed. Confidence is very different from certitude. Certitude is based on presumed "facts" and confidence is based on trust.

One observer noted, "Driving home from the city yesterday I was listening to a very interesting interview of Madeline Albright on NPR. Albright made a range of insightful observations about diplomacy, world affairs and the Presidency. During the course of the interview, one statement in particular jumped out at me. Albright said that she would rather have a President who was confident than a President who was certain. She noted that a confident President could take principled positions and stand for things that mattered, but would still have the good sense to listen to those around him and take counsel from a range of brilliant advisors. In contrast, a certain President would have no need for advisors because the appropriate course would be 'clear' to him."[13]

Certitude builds a protective wall around our faith, reinforced by "beliefs about. . ." Certitude exudes a fortress mentality. Confidence undergirds our faith, strengthens it from within, but doesn't attempt to defend our faith so that "nothing can get in." If I'm certain, I'm closed off. "Don't confuse me with the facts." If I'm confident, I delight in the truth at the heart of my life. Confidence causes me to be open to questions as they arise in my life.

- Certitude is closed off. Confidence is open-ended.

- Certitude is "fact-based." Confidence is "trust-based."

- Certitude knows. Confidence trusts.

- Certainty leads to intellectual and willful laziness. It's easier to be certain. But as a consequence, certainty shuts off an openness to learn.

- Certainty closes off anything new I have yet to consider. Confidence allows me to entertain new experiences and new learning.

- Certainty requires little faith. Confidence is built upon the depth of faith.

13. *VentureBlog,* April 10, 2008.

What about my marriage? My wife and I just celebrated our 50th wedding anniversary. Am I rock-solid certain that my marriage can survive any obstacle? Well, no, not exactly. I am confident that as we continue in our older years, we will walk together hand in hand. As some physical limitations appear, it has actually drawn us closer together. But in 1986, when a terrible auto accident caused a brain injury to my wife, our marriage barely survived even though we had an 18-month-old baby and a five-year-old child. So, I am confident about my marriage, but it would be foolish to be rock-solid certain. If certain, then I can take my relationship with my wife for granted. Confidence means that I must remain attentive as a husband. We're a "work in progress."

What about my role as a father? Am I rock-solid certain that I gave my children a fair start in life as a devoted father? No. We relocated across the country because of my career at critical points in their lives when it wasn't beneficial to them. They both struggled by these unwanted intrusions. Yet, I'm confident that I've been a positive role-model in their lives. I've made time for them and never neglected them. But if I was rock-solid certain, then I could step back from my relationship with them now that they are adults.

I can be confident in my faith and still accept the fact that life is filled with ambiguity, paradox and mystery. Certainty has no place for ambiguity, paradox, or mystery.

Horatio Spafford was a wealthy lawyer and landowner in Chicago. Yet, he suffered several traumatic events in his life. The first was the death of his four-year-old son and then the Great Chicago Fire of 1871 extensively damaged much of the property in which he had invested. He decided to travel to Europe in 1873, but he was delayed due to business concerns in Chicago. So, his wife and four daughters boarded the ship and while crossing the Atlantic, their ship collided with another and only Spafford's wife was spared. All four of his daughters drowned. Spafford raced to board a ship for Europe to join his grieving wife. When his ocean journey passed near the site of the collision, he was inspired to write the words to the beloved hymn, "It Is Well with My Soul." The beginning lyrics are:

> When peace like a river, attendeth my way,
> When sorrows like sea billows roll,
> Whatever my lot, Thou has taught me to say,
> "It is well, it is well, with my soul." (1873)

After such staggering losses, it is doubtful that Spafford could be certain of anything. But he could express his confidence in God, even when the circumstances of life were utterly absurd.

Thaler Pekar wrote in the Stanford Social Innovation Review, "Confidence invites a listener into conversation, whereas certainty shuts down conversation. Certainty excludes mutuality. Confidence allows for curiosity, and opens us to learning and growth. . . Confidence allows for fallibility and flexibility. . ."[14]

There is such a thing as over-confidence which might be akin to certainty. But healthy confidence offers us courage and strength to take on life's most difficult challenges.

If we look at the passage (Mark 7:25–30) about Jesus and the Syrophoenician woman, we see that it is the woman who leads this passage. Jesus responds to her initiative. Jesus is confident in this conversation, sharing the truth as he knows it, first proclaiming that his mission is solely to the children of Israel and not to Gentiles.

But Jesus is not certain. If so, he would have continued resisting the woman's request. If certain, he wouldn't have buckled at the mother's persistence. Certain, he would have turned her away assured that she was wrong and he was right.

Confident in his faith, he was able to listen to this woman, hear her, even though what she was saying seemed at right angles from what he thought to be true. If we can say anything about this passage it is that Jesus was able to change his mind and broaden his perspective. Yet, he wasn't wishy-washy. He wasn't a push-over. He exuded confidence but not certainty. This allowed him to respond to this woman, heal her daughter, and realize that his mission in life was far broader than he ever imagined.

Confidence is necessary and healthy.

Jesus approached the final chapter of his earthly life with confidence, not certitude. He was clearly shaken at the Last Supper, appearing fixated to talk with his disciples about one of them betraying his deep trust. He was clearly questioning in the Garden of Gethsemane, praying that God might remove the terrible choices of the next day. We also see him shaken on the cross, as he cried out to God, whom he felt had forsaken him in that moment of excruciating pain.

But in each closing episode of his earthly journey, he relied on faith, evidence of his confidence that God knew best, no matter the personal cost. "Nevertheless, not my will but Thine be done."

This confidence of faith was with Jesus throughout his earthly journey. We might assume that such confidence came without struggle for Jesus, since "he and the Father were one." (John 10:30) Yet, on several occasions, Jesus made clear to his disciples that he did not possess the full vision of his

14. Pekar, "Certainty versus Confidence," Jan. 11, 2013.

Father in Heaven. He also was looking through a mirror dimly. We see this when he responded to the rich young ruler who addressed him as "Good Teacher." And Jesus said, "Why do you call me good? No one is good but God alone." (Mark 10:18)

We see this when Jesus spoke of what only God knows: "But about that day and hour no one knows, neither the angels of heaven, nor the Son, but only the Father. . ." (Matt 24:36, Mark 13:32)

We see this when two of his disciples had asked for special privilege, and Jesus spoke of the limit of his spiritual power compared to God: ". . .to sit at my right hand or at my left is not mine to grant, but it is for those for whom it has been prepared by my Father." (Matt 20:23)

Throughout his life, Jesus is our model for confident, trusting faith.

What about Jesus?

What about Jesus? Was he a learner? If he was a human being, then he certainly was a learner. If he was God, or even the Son of God, would this have made him omniscient, and therefore, he had no reason to learn?

Was Jesus fully actualized into God's destiny when he was born, already fully wise and insightful? Had he already *Arrived*? If one reads the Gospels superficially, it might suggest that Jesus had no reason or cause to learn. He already "knew-it-all." He performed supernatural healings and miracles from Day One and had a foretaste of what the future held. However, a more careful reading of the Gospels may lead to a different conclusion.

Wouldn't it be peculiar if Jesus "knew everything," but hadn't the slightest idea what it meant to learn anything? If so, it would be a rather substantive difference between himself and all other human beings. And how can you "know everything" but know nothing about learning? Can you be a teacher if you have never experienced learning?

One of the greatest challenges for young preachers is to learn that you cannot preach what you haven't experienced. And while every sermon need not include personal narrative, it is very clear in listening to a sermon when the topic is foreign to the preacher. If the sermon doesn't push the preacher, doesn't challenge the preacher, or doesn't speak to the preacher, how on earth will it speak to or challenge others? And the same can be said for teachers. If a teacher keeps her subject matter at arm's length, then information may be transmitted but not real learning. Parker Palmer wrote, "Bad teachers distance themselves from their students. Good teachers join self and subject and students in the fabric of life. Good teachers possess a capacity for connectedness. They are able to weave a web of connections among themselves, their subjects, and their students so that students can learn to weave a world for themselves."[15]

As all good teachers, Jesus taught the importance of learning. He told his disciples, ". . .you are not to be called rabbi, for you have one teacher, and you are all students." (Matt 23:8) In Jesus' perspective, we are students, learners, all of us. Jesus taught the importance of learning, often in small one- and two-word lessons: "Receive!" (Mark 10:14) "Keep Alert!" (Mark 13:33) "Keep awake!" (Mark 13:37; 14:38) "Have your lamps lit!" (Luke 12:30) "Be Ready!" (Luke 12:40) "Pay attention. . ." (Luke 8:18a) "Let anyone with ears to hear, listen!" (Luke 14:35b) "Do you still not perceive or understand? Are you hearts hardened? Do you have eyes and fail to see? Do you have ears, and fail to hear? And do you not remember?" (Mark 8:17b-18) These are messages of a teacher to learners.

Has there ever been, in the history of the universe, a great teacher who was herself disengaged from learning? There are arrogant teachers, but they fail the test of greatness.

As I read the Gospels, I am convinced that there is an underlying assumption of Jesus as a learner. While the Gospels don't say, "Jesus learned something today," it was impossible to have witnessed what he witnessed and experienced what he experienced without learning something about himself, about his destiny, about his call, and about his God. *We follow Jesus not only because he is our teacher but also because he was an eager learner.*

Jesus was a learner. We are learners.
Do you follow Jesus in your learning?

I believe that Jesus had to find his way just as we must find our way. The Gospels describe his difficult choices and costly crossroads. He had to ask, as do we, "What will happen if I choose this path?" There are many examples of this, but one time, just before the Festival of Booths, Jesus had to decide whether to remain in Galilee or enter Judea. And his own brothers urged him, "Leave Galilee and go to Judea so that your disciples may see the works you are doing; for no one who wants to be widely known acts in secret. If you do these things, show yourself to the world." (John 7:3f.) Jesus felt that a grand entry into Jerusalem was ill-timed and argued with his brothers. Eventually, he decided upon a quieter entrance during the Festival.

Did Jesus face difficult choices and stand at costly crossroads?
Or did everything just fall in his lap?

15. Palmer, *The Courage to Teach*, 11.

Did Jesus possess wisdom from God as he tied together the loose ends of his life? Yes, certainly. He had to be a reflective person, just like his mother (Luke 2:19; 2:51). At mid-point in his ministry, he began to understand more fully his destiny and how he fit into God's eternal plan. For starters, he learned something about the meaning of suffering.

As a white person, I have to listen to persons of color to recognize my privilege and the tragic costs of racism. Without their perspective, I am blinded to reality.

Think about it: how can you "know" something unless you learned it?

You cannot know the meaning of suffering unless you have suffered. You cannot know the meaning of love unless you have loved. You cannot know the true meaning of poverty, unless you've been poor. If you were born into wealth and privilege and have known nothing else, then you cannot possibly know what it means to be hungry, or to lack shelter, or to be unable to provide for your family at the most basic level.

In my first pastorate, I worked in a team ministry. And the other two pastors with whom I was serving were away on vacation when an older member died. I had never met this woman and knew nothing about her. Worse, I had never attended a funeral and knew nothing about death or grief. Because of my inexperience, I was at a complete loss to know how to be a pastor to this woman's family or what to say at her funeral. I asked for a second meeting with the family in which I explained my inexperience and offered to find a more experienced pastor to lead their mother's funeral. They would have nothing of it, and so I learned "on the job" how to conduct a funeral with a very nervous funeral director guiding me! We human beings are woefully ill-prepared without prior experience upon which to draw.

Thank God, I was about sixteen years into my ministry before I had to support a family through the death of their new-born child. I was woefully ill-prepared for that tragedy. I had never experienced anything approximating that kind of loss. I had no base of experience upon which to draw except my deep sadness and grief at that moment. Trying to find my way through that experience as a pastor with dear friends who were the grieving parents, it was a steep learning curve. Thankfully, I haven't had too many experiences of the death of a child, but I was better prepared for the few that followed because those first parents were mature and articulate with their feelings. I learned from them. No one can deny that we can learn from our experiences.

Some may argue, "If the Gospels never speak of Jesus learning, doesn't that settle the issue?" Yet, the Gospels never state that Jesus laughed, or smiled, but isn't it nearly impossible to consider this man who so enjoyed life never laughing or smiling? When Jesus was holding babies and blessing them, would it have been possible to do so sternly?

> *The Gospels never state that Jesus smiled.*
> *Don't you believe that he did?*

The Gospels reveal much about Jesus: that he wept, that he experienced great anxiety, that he had a great need to go off by himself for prayer, and that he felt exhaustion. And the Gospels reveal that Jesus was an active learner. In two places, Luke speaks of Jesus learning and growing in wisdom and stature (Luke 2:40 and 2:52). Luke speaks with the same language about John the Baptist learning and growing (Luke 1:80).

Jesus learned from Zacchaeus and Levi, tax collectors, and their surprising receptivity.

He learned from the Syrophoenician woman, who insisted that he take her seriously.

He learned from his deep conversation with the Samaritan woman at the well.

He learned from the Samaritan leper who returned to him giving thanks.

He learned from John the Baptist.

He learned from his mother, Mary.

He learned from the scholars in the Temple when he was twelve years old.

He learned from Peter's declaration, "You are the Messiah!"

To take away Jesus' capacity as a learner is the same as stripping him of his humanity. In truth, it makes Jesus "less than us" rather than "more than us," which I presume is the intent of such a belief.

So we come to the question with which I have long struggled, "Why do some Christians prefer an 'Arrived Jesus' to a 'Becoming Jesus'?" An "Arrived Jesus" implies that Jesus' life had already arrived at his destination from the moment he was born in his Bethlehem crib. It implies that God designed a tight script for Jesus' life. This conclusion implies that Jesus faced no true crossroads in his life and no decisions that could have changed his life's trajectory. He didn't need to be baptized, he wasn't really tempted in the wilderness, he didn't need to cry at the death of Lazarus, he didn't need to feel anxious in the Garden of Gethsemane, and he didn't need to be in anguish on the cross. In short, if Jesus had already arrived, why feel any emotion at all? Everything in his life was scripted and pre-planned, right down to each moment.

If so, Jesus lived the ultimate predestined life. No courage was required. No risk was involved. No question ever asked. No decisions needed.

Yet, this doesn't describe a human being, does it? It prescribes a robotic understanding of Jesus' life. In other words, he really wasn't so remarkable because, as if on auto-pilot, he methodically followed God's tight script. Jesus lived the ultimate Easy Life!

Please! Give me a flesh-and-blood Jesus who faced challenges, decisions and crossroads throughout his life! Give me an eager Jesus who made new discoveries throughout his life! And at each significant moment, when he could have gone another direction, he courageously chose God's path. Give me a Jesus who worried, who showed anguish and fear, who mourned the loss of friends, who experienced great frustration, who was so filled with anguish in Gethsemane that sweat fell from his forehead like great drops of blood, who suffered humiliation and scorn, and who cried out from the cross in agony.

This is the Jesus whom the Gospels portray, not some angelic being hovering a foot above the earth, but a real, live human being who shows us how to be real live human beings!

None of this contradicts that Jesus was called to become the Son of God! Not at all! That surely was in God's mind and heart when Jesus was born, but Jesus had to journey to accept and fulfill this calling. And that is what makes him such a compelling human being, such a complete human being, and a magnificent example for the rest of us.

Give me a "Becoming Jesus" any day! This is the "Jesus" portrayed in the Gospels.

Jesus' Awakening Moments

All human beings require daily periods of sleep and rest as well as daily periods awake and actively engaged. If we deprive ourselves of either for an extended period of time, we pay the price. But there is also a metaphorical way of speaking of being asleep and awake. We can suddenly wake up to the cries of people who have been unsuccessfully trying to get our attention. We can fall asleep so as not to be alert or awake to the possibilities around us. The prophet Isaiah recorded these words: "Morning by morning, (the Lord God) wakens—wakens my ear to listen as those who are taught. The Lord God has opened my ear. . ." (Isa 50:4c-5a)

Waking up, metaphorically, was one of Jesus' most important messages. "Be on your guard, stay awake. . ." "Be Ready. . ." "Be alert. . ." (Matt 24:42; 25:13; Mark 13:33; Luke 12:40) These were messages important to him because of the awakening moments in his life.

At various points in his life, Jesus awakened to God's special destiny for his life:

- In his Temple presentation at the age of 12, by asking questions of and listening to the Temple leaders; his realization that he was "at home" in "God's House"

- In his baptism in the River Jordan by John, in which Jesus heard the Holy Spirit speak of his unique role

- In the wilderness temptations which stiffened his resolve and clarified his intentions

- Upon his first return to Nazareth in which he used Isaiah's writing to share his own personal ministry statement

- In Gethsemane, where he faltered with fear and anxiety before mustering his courage; ". . .let this cup pass away from me. *Nevertheless*, let your will be done. . ." (Luke 22:42, NJB) "Nevertheless" signifies his growing spiritual insight. It was a long agonizing "nevertheless."

- On the cross, where he experienced God's absence and overcame it.

These are all presented as "wake-up" moments in Jesus' life. He emerged from each challenge growing in awareness and willingness to be all that God called him to be. If we look closely, Jesus *grew* into his role. He wasn't fully "there" at the beginning. Certainly not as a lad at 12—precocious, certainly, but not the full revelation of God.

What are your awakening moments?

He was on a journey. And like most of us, Jesus could have veered away from God's path at any critical crossroad. Thank God, he did not and the result is the most incredible human life ever lived—a life that became a window through which we see God's love most clearly. We have seen the light "of the glory of God in the face of Jesus Christ." (2 Cor 4:6)

The Nazarenes Tell Us a Lot

There is one story, told in all three Synoptic Gospels (Matt 13:54–58; Mark 6:1–6a; Luke 4:16–30), that offers amazing insight into Jesus' learning and becoming. It is the story of Jesus, after he first left Nazareth, returning to his hometown. This was one interaction that did not go well for Jesus, ending, incredibly, with his fellow Nazarenes trying to end his life by "hurling him off a nearby cliff."

One might assume that when Jesus returned to his hometown, a small village of maybe 400 people, he would receive a heroes' welcome. At first, the visit appeared to be going well. "All spoke well of him and were amazed at the gracious words that came from his mouth." (Luke 4:22) Luke places Jesus' return to Nazareth as one of his first acts upon returning to Galilee. This placement likely speaks of a close affinity Jesus felt toward his home town where he had grown up.

Yet, the Nazarenes raised many questions about Jesus, which all three synoptic authors quote liberally:

- The Nazarenes were "amazed at (his) gracious words. . ." (Luke 4:22)
- "Is not this Joseph's son?" (Luke 4:22c)
- "Where did this man get this wisdom and these deeds of power?" (Matt 13:54)
- "Is not this the carpenter's son? Is not his mother called Mary? And are not his brothers James and Joseph and Simon and Judas? And are not all his sisters with us?" (Matt 13:55–56a)
- "Where then did this man get all this?" (Matt 13:56b)
- Many who heard him in Nazareth "were astounded." (Mark 6:2c)
- "Where did this man get all this? (Mark 6:22b)
- "What is this wisdom that has been given to him? (Mark 6:2c)
- "What deeds of power are being done by his hands!" (Mark 6:2d)
- "Is not this the carpenter, the son of Mary and brother of James and Joses and Judas and Simon, and are not his sisters here with us?" (Mark 6:3)

The authors of Matthew and Mark seem compelled to repeat the point with repetitive questions, in Matthew, six questions and in Mark, four questions. What seems clear is that the Nazarenes were having trouble recognizing Jesus upon his return. He appeared unfamiliar to them. It wasn't likely that his physical appearance had changed. But it does suggest that from the time Jesus left Nazareth as a young adult, until his return at the beginning or in the midst of his ministry, he had changed so much that the Nazarenes were having trouble reconciling the "Jesus" they knew growing up with the "Jesus" who now appeared in their synagogue.

The fact that Mark states that Jesus is "the carpenter" and that he is the "son of Mary," suggests that Joseph was deceased. Joseph was the village carpenter and taught the trade to Jesus. Jesus and his mother shared the perspective that Jesus had a mission far greater than remaining a carpenter in Nazareth. But as the eldest son, he had a moral responsibility to care for his mother and their large family (at least four brothers and multiple sisters). The next oldest son was James, who became the leader of the early church in Jerusalem after Jesus' death and resurrection. So, his next oldest brother had strong leadership potential.

I had always assumed that Jesus remained in Nazareth until he was nearly 30, and then he left, was subsequently baptized and tempted, and returned to Galilee, all in relatively short order. But in the reaction of the Nazarenes, I now realize that Jesus couldn't have been gone just a few months. For their reaction to make sense, Jesus had to have left Nazareth some years before. And while away, the Holy Spirit led him through an amazing season of personal transformation as to make him unrecognizable to those who knew him before.

Jesus left Galilee and went into the wilderness to meet John the Baptist. For the Jews, the wilderness was a place of spirituality, a place of identity-formation, a place of personal cleansing and resolve. God speaks from the wilderness with greater clarity. Where else would Jesus go?

As amazing as Jesus' gifts were, still, he could not have developed such alternative, sophisticated theological ideas in Nazareth, which had no school of advanced study. His natural gifts were evident at the age of 12 in the Temple, but still he needed a social climate where his thoughts could be challenged, deepened, and reach full expression. John and his community of disciples likely provided this context. Jesus witnessed and experienced a master and his disciples living in community at the edge of the wilderness. It was the perfect learning environment for Jesus.

Matthew quotes John the Baptist (3:11) saying, ". . .but one more powerful than I is coming after me." This phrase, "after me," is normally used denoting discipleship. In Matt 4:19, the Greek literally says, "*Come after me and I will make you fishers of men.*" The New Jerusalem Bible and the New American Bible translate the Greek in this way. If so, John is stating that Jesus was with him as his disciple. The dialogue between them in Matthew makes more sense if they had significant time together before Jesus' baptism. Therefore, Jesus was in a learning and receiving position with John the Baptist. John was a mentor to him, one to whom he owed much, and one from whom he learned much.

I had one spiritual teacher who had an incredible influence upon me. I didn't meet her until after seminary. I had wonderful professors in seminary but it was Emma Lou Benignus who stretched me spiritually, a woman from whom I gained *Spiritual Expanse*. Every time I was with her, never for long periods of time, I experienced an opening to the Spirit that had a lasting influence upon me. Particularly in disciplines of prayer and meditation, Emma Lou was my teacher like no one else.

I have had the privilege of mentoring nearly twenty young people studying for ministry. There was one young woman who came to me as a medical doctor from Mexico. I immediately recognized in her uncommon gifts for ministry. She came to the United States to study in seminary so that she could become a medical missionary.

I was her mentor for two years, longer than any other intern. I remember one season in which I was training her to preach. I had such confidence in her but I realized that there was something in her sermons that seemed detached from her own experience. One week, I asked her to deliver her upcoming sermon with me sitting alone in the sanctuary. I pushed her. She went home and re-developed her sermon and delivered it again. Throughout that week, I kept pushing her. There was no "her" in her sermon. Finally, she was in tears, but only after the tears did she deliver one of the most incredible sermons I've ever heard. Finally, the sermon applied not only to the rest of us but also to her.

I realized at the time that her ministry would be far more global and wide-reaching than mine would ever be. And indeed, that has become true. She is now a director of global ministries throughout Latin America and I often hear of her far-reaching impact and her theological insight. Though obviously on a different scale, I can imagine what John felt with his student, Jesus. John once said of Jesus, as an admiring teacher of his prize pupil, "He must grow greater, I must grow less." (John 3:30 NJB)

One prominent New Testament scholar, James M. Robinson, goes so far as to title one chapter in a recent book, "Jesus Was Converted by John," and argues that Jesus didn't gain a sense of call until he came to John. The two eventually went their separate ways. John followed a method of retreat and disengagement from society (much like the Essenes). Jesus created a different way of engaging mainstream society with a subversive message. While their messages and approaches were different, there appears little doubt that John had a profound impact upon Jesus at a "teachable moment" in his life.[16] Jesus said of John the Baptist, speaking as a student to his teacher, "Truly, I tell you among those born of women no one has arisen greater than John the Baptist. . ." (Matt 11:11) And John said of Jesus, "I baptize you with water; but one who is more powerful that I is coming; I am not worthy

---

16. Robinson, *The Gospel of Jesus*, 111.

to untie the thong of his sandals." (Luke 3:16) For the years they were learning together, Jesus gained in wisdom, ethical stature, and maturity. He developed a deepening understanding of what God was asking of him.

John had already discerned that God was soon to introduce the Promised One. John was on the look-out and he eventually recognized in Jesus the coming Messiah. He no doubt helped Jesus understand his role in this divine destiny.

One sign of the high regard Jesus had for John occurred when Jesus learned that Herod had beheaded John. The Gospel of Matthew states, "Now when Jesus heard (that John had been beheaded), he withdrew from there in a boat to a deserted place by himself." (14:13a) The Gospel of Mark even states that Jesus did not launch his Galilean ministry until after John was arrested. "Now after John was arrested, Jesus came to Galilee, proclaiming the good news of God. . ." (1:14) This could suggest that when John was arrested, Jesus realized he could no longer delay the launch of his ministry.

It is interesting that Jesus never attempted to replace John, nor did he attempt to take over John's community after John's death. Jesus formed his own group of followers which he built upon the principles he learned from John. But the two teachers had different mandates and a different mission.

This mentoring season had to have reached its climax in Jesus' baptism by John in the River Jordan. This is recorded by all the Gospel writers as a *Turning Point* in his life. In his baptism, he received the ultimate blessing from God: "And a voice came from heaven: 'You are my Son, the Beloved, with you I am well pleased." (Luke 3:22b)

It was likely during this time in study and reflection that Jesus chose Isaiah 61:1–2a as his personal mission statement. It was a mission statement that he chose to share first and only with the Nazarenes and then to proclaim, "Today this scripture has been fulfilled in your hearing." (Luke 4:21)

Matthew includes a dialogue between Jesus and John, just prior to his being baptized:

"John would have prevented Jesus' baptism, saying, 'I need to be baptized by you, and do you come to me?' But Jesus answered him, 'Let it be so now; for it is proper for us in this way to fulfill all righteousness.' Then John consented." (3:14–15) This dialogue reveals several things:

a. John had already spent sufficient time with Jesus to recognize Jesus' extraordinary faith and magnetism

b. These two teachers had an honest, natural pattern of communication

c. They both recognized that Something beyond them was shaping this moment

d. John was still in the position of authority; he could baptize Jesus or prevent his baptism

e. But there was a power shift occurring in their relationship; John is the baptizer but Jesus emerged from the water with a unique call and a larger mission separate from John's

f. John embraced Jesus' unique mission

g. John was the baptizer; Jesus didn't baptize people—he let his disciples baptize. Jesus found other rites and symbols to represent his message and mission.

There is a passage in Luke (20:1–8) during the last week of Jesus' life that points to John's influence upon Jesus. Jesus had just "cleansed the temple," an extremely provocative action threatening the temple's economic system. This system directly benefited the chief priests, scribes and elders of the people. "One day, as Jesus was teaching the people in the temple and telling the good news, the chief priests and the scribes came with the elders and said to him, 'Tell us, by what authority are you doing these things? Who is it who gave you this authority?'" (Luke 20:1–2) They were questioning him because of his lack of formal training under a recognized teacher/rabbi. The formal training and credentialing of rabbi's had not yet developed this early in the first century, but "it would have been common for one to establish his authority by citing the tradition of one of his teachers. Paul, for example, could say that he was 'brought up in this city at the feet of Gamaliel, educated strictly according to ancestral law' (Acts 22:3)."[17]

Jesus easily understood their question: Where are your credentials? Under what rabbinical leader did you study? "Who gave you this authority?" And he answered their question by citing the credibility and authority of John the Baptist. Jesus' authority rested with John the Baptist and because John was so popular with the people, Jesus silenced his critics. John was not a recognized rabbinical teacher. He was not one with the authority to educate new rabbis. But he was recognized by the people as a prophet from God. And therein rested Jesus authority: upon John as a contemporary prophet from God.

It is important to choose your teachers wisely. Jesus could have gone to the scribes in Jerusalem. He could have gone to one of the leading rabbis of his day and asked to be a disciple during a training period. Either of these would have been the more traditional, established path. Had he followed this course, no one ever would have asked, "How does this man have such learning, when he has never been taught?" (John 7:15b) People were aware

17. *The New Interpreter's Bible*, Vol. 9, 377.

that Jesus lacked the credentials and authority which a recognized and established teacher could provide. Yet, it is clear from Jesus' interaction with the scholars in Jerusalem that he was an outsider.

When it came time for me to go to college, I cannot say that I selected the school I would attend. Nearly all my aunts, uncles, and both parents attended William Jewell College, and my sister was entering her junior year there when I entered as a freshman. I just followed the family tradition and never considered another school. When it came time for me to decide on a seminary, I was eager to select my own school. I was an American Baptist by that point, and we had three progressive seminaries in the East and I flew to all three campuses on one extended trip to meet faculty, administrators, and students. I also visited a United Church of Christ seminary in Chicago. I carefully explored each possibility trying to discover what kind of graduates these schools produced. I was choosing my teachers carefully. In the end, I narrowed my search to two schools, Colgate Rochester Divinity School and Crozer Theological Seminary. I chose Colgate Rochester in late Spring and by June, Crozer unexpectedly decided to close its campus and relocate to Colgate Rochester Crozer Divinity School. So I received the best of both worlds. It felt like I had chosen wisely.

Jesus also chose his teacher wisely. He turned from the traditional path of Jewish study in the first century which was centered in Jerusalem and around the temple. Instead, he chose a subversive, non-traditional teacher in John the Baptist. There are great similarities between the ministries of John and Jesus, though also startling differences. But the message of repentance was at the heart of both of their teachings.

Following his baptism, Jesus was driven by the Holy Spirit into the wilderness, further than he had ever dared to go. And he met the Devil in the wilderness. He met Temptation in the wilderness. He encountered an alternative path to the one toward which God had been preparing him. If he chose, he could perform miracles to feed himself, to take good care of himself. He could build an empire upon his own dashing personality and power. He could compete with God Himself.

Each of these three temptations had to have had a transforming impact upon Jesus. To turn away from self-gratifying needs, and turn toward God in all humility, had to be life-changing. Just as his baptism with John was life-changing. Just as his taking to heart this seminal passage from Isaiah was life-changing. Just as the years he spent studying with and learning from John were life-changing. These were his years of Spiritual Expanse. He experienced God's *metanoia*, a turning or re-orienting of his life toward God. Metanoia means a transforming change of heart.

Jesus became a New Person under the tutelage of God, the Holy Spirit, and John's community. Only after such a powerful season of transformation and conversion could Jesus have returned to Nazareth and be nearly unrecognizable to them: "Isn't this Mary and Joseph's son?"

My sister is two years older and was two years ahead of me in school. In a small school district, we would often pass through the same classes and teachers. My sister seemed to me like a nearly perfect student, well-behaved, responsible, and attentive. And then I came along. It was almost predictable, after about 3 weeks in the school year, that the teacher would take me aside and ask, "Aren't you Marcia's brother?" The teachers already knew the answer. They knew my father and mother. They knew we were a family. But her behavior and my behavior were so different that it prompted the question, "Are you really your sister's brother?"

"Isn't this Mary and Joseph's son?" It seems likely that the Nazarenes were resentful of these changes in Jesus which they had no role in causing. You can almost hear the Nazarenes saying, "He shows up in our village, after all these years, and he has a sense of authority that he didn't have growing up among us. He has a sense of confidence that God is working through him that we didn't recognize. He has a divine mission in his life that we couldn't see."

At first, the Nazarenes were "amazed at his gracious words," but that quickly changed. No doubt from his participation in Sabbath readings throughout his young adult years, the Nazarenes often felt pushed by Jesus' expansive questions and insights. And now he came to them with the audacity to state that when Jews had hardened hearts, God sent Elijah to a foreigner, a widow in Sidon. And though there were many lepers in Israel at the time, God didn't heal one Jewish leper but instead healed Naaman, a Syrian! God preferred foreigners to Jews! God worked through heathens rather than the Righteous! God healed no men but a foreign woman!

This was too much for the Nazarene elders of this remote Jewish enclave. They felt they needed to set an example with Jesus as a rogue teacher. To them, throwing Jesus off a cliff was not an over-reaction. They gave Jesus his beginning and they had the authority to bring his life to an end.

Jesus said, "Doubtless you will quote to me this proverb, 'Doctor, cure yourself!' And you will say, 'Do here also in your hometown the things that we have heard you did in Capernaum.' And he said, "Truly, I tell you, no prophet is accepted in the prophet's hometown." (Luke 4:23–24) Jesus may have never returned to Nazareth in the first place had he been aware of the hostility he would encounter. To our knowledge, it was his last visit home.

I think the questions of the Nazarenes suggest that they did not view Jesus as the Son of God or the Messiah during his growing-up years. They did not recognize a halo hanging over his head at 8, 18, or 25 years of age. They may have noticed remarkable gifts, but certainly not on this scale. Many of us tend to think that Jesus knew from birth the special role God intended for him, and that all the pieces of his life fell easily into place as if choreographed from heaven. We want to believe that he experienced no struggle, no crossroads, and that he simply followed God's tight script for his life. He was born an Arrived Jesus.

The Nazarene's questions suggest otherwise. He wasn't a prophet to them, or even a prophet-in-the-making. He wasn't the Messiah, or a Messiah-in-Waiting. He was not the Hope of their nation or the Savior of the Jews.

We can only surmise that Jesus underwent radical transformation during his years following his departure from Nazareth and his family. There was a "Before Nazareth" and an "After Nazareth" in Jesus' life. The Nazarenes utterly misread what God could do in Christ. "Isn't this Mary and Joseph's son?"

Do you have a "Before Nazareth" and an "After Nazareth" in your life?

Jesus wasn't just a human being. He was a human *becoming*, a person reaching for a flourishing life, not just for himself but for everyone he met. And that "Journey of Becoming" found its fullest expression in the years between his departure from Nazareth and his return to Nazareth.

We know these things happened while Jesus was away from Nazareth before launching his ministry:

- He spent time with John's community of disciples

- He was baptized by John

- He learned admiration and respect for John's calling

- He was exposed to John's radically inclusive message and audience

- His authority came from John who was widely perceived as a prophet of God

- He likely selected the Isaiah text as his personal mission statement

- He spent time in the wilderness deepening his resolve for God

- He received God's special calling for his life.

Since Jesus and John the Baptist were similar in age, one might wonder how John got a head-start with a fully-developed ministry before Jesus left Nazareth. Yet, their upbringings were radically different. John's father, Zechariah, was a priest, serving in the temple in nearby Jerusalem, giving John open access to the finest scholars of the nation and easy opportunities to study the Torah. Jesus, on the other hand, grew up in the remote outpost of Nazareth, where access to Jewish scholars was nonexistent. Jesus' family business was carpentry. John's family business was the temple. Likely, what John received from highly astute teachers and his own father-priest, Jesus received from John. Also, John's parents, Zechariah and Elizabeth, were quite elderly when he was born and when they died, John had no family responsibilities.

It seems that John rebelled against the aristocracy of the temple with their beautiful flowing robes and fortified positions of wealth and public respect. He began to dress and eat alternatively and left Jerusalem to take up residence in the wilderness, preaching a radically different message. He condemned the status quo and urged Israel to repent, to be baptized, and to live a repentant life.

If Jesus and John were related, and Jesus' family stayed with Elizabeth and Zechariah when on pilgrimages to Jerusalem, this affords Jesus opportunity to have been exposed to John's thinking while growing up. John's influence upon Jesus could have been from childhood on and explains why Jesus chose to go to John to be baptized and launch his ministry.

We see in young Jesus at the age of twelve an insatiable appetite to engage Israel's scholars when he stayed behind in Jerusalem just for the opportunity of engaging them. This story reminds us that Jesus had no opportunity in his remote corner of Galilee for such uplifting conversations. Jesus was eager for the kind of conversations that John could take for granted throughout his growing up years.

I add this last insight at the end of this chapter because it came to me after I had submitted this book for publication and was in the process of final edits.

When he emerged from his wilderness years, Jesus shared two things with the Nazarenes. First, he shared his "personal ministry statement" from Isaiah, proclaiming to them, "Today this scripture has been fulfilled in your hearing." (4:21) They received this proclamation "graciously." Later, he called himself a "prophet," a title he seldom used. "Truly, I tell you, no prophet is accepted in the prophet's hometown." (4:24) Isn't it possible that John the Baptist began his ministry in the Judean hills and faced rejection by his hometown friends and acquaintances? Could Jesus have learned this statement from John? People certainly considered John a prophet. Can't we hear Jesus asking John at one point in their time together, "Why did you leave your home in the beautiful hills? Why not stay among your own people?" And we can hear John answering, "No prophet is accepted in the prophet's hometown."

Next, Jesus taught the Nazarenes that God can work outside the Jews, through a Sidonese widow facing famine and by healing a Syrian leper. He made the point that there were plenty of Jewish widows nearby but God passed over them sending Elijah to a Gentile and plenty of Jewish lepers nearby but God passed over them sending Elisha to a Syrian.

This teaching instinctively and immediately repelled the Nazarenes, angering them to the point of threatening to end his life. "When they heard this, all in the synagogue were filled with rage." (4:28) This was the most offensive, most "non-Nazarene" teaching Jesus could have offered! The Nazarenes fiercely practiced an ethno-centric tribal faith.

Assuming this came soon after Jesus' years with John the Baptist, doesn't this passage suggest that this teaching also came from John? What was John teaching? What was he proclaiming? To whom was he proclaiming? His was a message of repentance. "Bear fruits worthy of repentance," he said to the crowds. (3:8) He said to the Jews, "Don't come to me bragging that you have Abraham as your ancestor." (3:8c) ". . .I tell you, God is able from these stones to raise up children to Abraham." (3:8d)

William Barclay in his commentary on this passage writes, "The Jews had not the slightest doubt that in God's economy there was a most favoured nation clause. They held that God would judge the nations with one standard but the Jews with another. They, in fact, held that a man was safe from judgment simply in virtue of the fact that he was a Jew. A son of Abraham was exempt from judgment. John told them that racial privilege meant nothing. . ."[18]

Who were in these crowds? "Even tax collectors came to be baptized. . ." (3:12) This had to have been eye-opening to young Jesus, his first encounter with repentant tax collectors! And it had to prepare Jesus for his later interactions with Zacchaeus, Levi, and other repentant tax collectors. And "soldiers" also came to him. (3:14) Who were these soldiers? Jewish? Or could they have been Gentiles? Local mercenaries serving under Herod? Matthew broadens the group coming to John, ". . .many Pharisees and Sadducees (were) coming for baptism. . ." (Matt 3:7) Could eunuchs also have come? Could women? Could prostitutes? Matthew states that "the tax collectors and the prostitutes believed. . ." in John the Baptist. (Matt 21:32b) At one point it is reported that John ". . .penetrated

---

18. Barclay, *The Gospel of Luke, The Daily Study Bible Series,* 29.

north-westward into Samaria and baptized within a few miles of its well-populated towns."[19] (John 3:23)

In other words, John called sinners as well as the so-called righteous to repentance, and crowds of all kinds came to John to be baptized. Could John have been the source of this controversial insight about Elijah and Elisha? Jesus certainly did not learn it from the Nazarenes! And if this insight blew the minds of the Nazarenes, wouldn't it also have blown Jesus' mind when he first heard it? He had never in his life heard anything like this as it was completely counter to the "wisdom" of the Nazarenes, or, for that matter, the common wisdom among the Galileans. This insight surely came from a non-Galilean source. John the Baptist was the likely source.

John had a boundary-busting ministry, calling any and all people to repentance. Jesus took that boundary-busting message to Nazareth and his hometown people were enraged by it. "The people of Jesus' hometown read the Scriptures as promises of God's exclusive covenant with them, a covenant that involved promises of deliverance from their oppressors. Jesus came announcing deliverance, but it was not a national deliverance but God's promise of liberation for all the poor and oppressed regardless of nationality, gender, or race. When the radical inclusiveness of Jesus' announcement became clear to those gathered in the synagogue in Nazareth, their commitment to their own community boundaries took precedence over their joy that God had sent a prophet among them. In the end, because they were not open to the prospect of others' sharing in the bounty of God's deliverance, they themselves were unable to receive it."[20]

John stands prominently in the background of Jesus' return visit to Nazareth. The message of these two Jewish prophets did not sit well with the Nazarenes.

25 Gospel Instances of Jesus Learning

In the Gospels, we have no fewer than 25 examples of Jesus as a learner:

1. In the birth stories of Matthew and Luke, the story is told from the vantage of what Jesus would become in his life, not what he would accomplish on the day of his birth. Joseph experienced an angel of the Lord appearing to him "in a dream and said, 'Joseph, son of David, do not be afraid to take Mary as your wife, for the child conceived in her is from the Holy Spirit. She will bear a son, and you are to name him Jesus, for he will

---

19. *The Interpreter's Dictionary of the Bible*, Vol. 2, 961.

20. R. Alan Culpepper, *The New Interpreter's Bible*, Volume IX, 108.

save his people from their sins." (Matt 1:20–21) *He will save* is future tense: this will occur as Jesus grows and fulfills his destiny.

The same tense is found in the Gospel of Luke, when the angel Gabriel appeared to Mary: ". . .you will conceive in your womb and bear a son, and you will name him Jesus. He *will be great,* and *will be called* the Son of the Most High, and the Lord God *will give to him* the throne of his ancestor David. *He will reign* over the house of Jacob forever. . ." (Luke 1:31–33a)

This is all future tense, of what will unfold as Jesus grows, matures, and fulfills God's special destiny for his life.

2 From the start of Luke's Gospel, found in Luke 2:40 and Luke 2:52, the same clear message is repeated that Jesus was a learner! "And as the child grew to maturity, he was filled with wisdom and God's favor was upon him." (NJB, Luke 2:40) "And as Jesus continued to grow in body and in mind, he grew also in the love of God and of those who knew him." (Luke 2:52, Philipps Modern English) "Jesus grew" is repeated in both verses, though the Greek word is different in each verse. In verse 40, it literally means "continue to grow" and in verse 52, "to advance or progress."

Traditional commentaries make the same point: *(Ellicott's Commentary for English Readers)* "The soul of Jesus was human, i.e., subject to the conditions and limitations of human knowledge, and learnt as others learn." "With Him, as with others, wisdom widened with the years, and came into His human soul through the same channels and by the same processes as into the souls of others—instruction, e.g., in the school of Nazareth, and attendance at its synagogue. . ." *(Expositor's Greek Testament)* He "steadily grew. . .in wisdom. . .and in stature, both growth alike real." *(Bengel's Gnomen)* "He progressed in accordance with or in respect to human nature, and the wisdom of human nature. . ." *(Cambridge Bible for Schools and Colleges)* "The growth of our Lord is here described as a natural human growth." *(Pulpit Commentary)* ". . .St. Luke evidently understands the humanity of Jesus as a reality. . . . . .the Boy learnt as others learnt, subject to the ordinary growth and development of human knowledge. . ."

We should also note that Luke 1:80 uses the same language to describe John the Baptist as a child: "The child grew and became strong in spirit. . ."

Jesus and John the Baptist both entered the world starting as all human babies with much to learn. Jesus "learnt as others learn," "a natural human growth."

3 I have often wondered why Jesus didn't begin his ministry until the age of 30 (Luke 3:23). This was considerably later in the first-century lifespan than ours. Many thirty-year-old's in our society are still "finding themselves."

But with a shorter lifespan, much of Jesus' life would have already passed by the age of thirty. Why begin so late? Why not launch his ministry at the age of twenty? The logical explanation is that Jesus wasn't yet ready to fulfill the profound calling God laid before him. God would send Jesus out on his mission when Jesus was ready. Jesus had a lot of learning and preparation to do before launching his public ministry. Jesus started his ministry with many amazing ideas already developed and theological insights different from other Jewish teachers of his day. Without formal education from a respected rabbi, he had to develop and defend these provocative ideas. That he did so in his first thirty years is nothing short of remarkable! Some of this learning happened while growing up in Nazareth and even more after he left for the Judean wilderness.

4 Why was Jesus baptized by John? The earliest Gospel, Mark, offers little narrative: "In those days Jesus came from Nazareth of Galilee and was baptized by John in the River Jordan." (1:9) John's baptism was for "repentance for the forgiveness of sins." Luke sticks close to Mark's version, ". . .when Jesus had also been baptized and was praying, the heaven was opened. . ." (3:21)

Nearly all agree that Jesus was baptized by John because it was necessary as he turned from his private life in Nazareth to launch his public ministry. His baptism was his rite of passage from Preparation to Practice, from Study to Engagement.

Finally, evidence that John the Baptist mattered a great deal to Jesus is found in the way Jesus responded to John's untimely and violent death. If John was just a competing teacher, Jesus might have felt some relief. But John was clearly his mentor, and his death left Jesus feeling alone, anxious, and grieved. (Matt 14:11–13)

5 Read Matthew 15:21–28; Mark 7:25–30—Many scholars have pointed to his interaction with the Syrophoenician woman as an example of Jesus learning. The woman came to him, begging for mercy for her daughter, "But Jesus did not answer her at all." (23a) He explained his disinterest: "I was sent only to the lost sheep of the house of Israel." ((24) With her, he called Gentiles "dogs," which under any circumstance was derogatory. We would not expect this of Jesus. And instead of his leading the conversation, the woman took the initiative and opened his eyes to her faith, which up to that point he could not recognize. Only after this change in his perspective, was he able to respond to the woman with tenderness and healing love.

In this story, the woman essentially does not change. She comes to Jesus on faith and demands a response based on her trust in him. The one who changes is Jesus, who begins unresponsive, then unsympathetic, then sarcastic (at best), and only then, responsive to the woman. She stays the same. It is Jesus who changes.

One question to ask: why is this episode included in two of the Gospels? It surely does not show Jesus at his best, but rather repeating prejudices and stereotypes of his day. And the "teacher" in this episode is not Jesus, but the Gentile woman. This shows a willingness on the part of the gospel writers to reveal the humanity of Jesus and his ability to change (and learn) when faced with new situations.

It is incredulous to see what some commentators do with this text, often suggesting that the dialogue between Jesus and the Canaanite woman was inserted later by the church for its own purposes. Or that Jesus was teasing the woman and wasn't really serious. Or that he was testing the woman to determine the depth of her faith. Others suggest that the word Jesus used was for small dogs as loveable pets in order to moderate the hostility in their dialogue. But this is a modern view of pets. In historical context, "dog" was an insulting term used by Jews (I Sam 17:43; Prov 26:11; Eccl 9:4; Isa 56:10–11; Matt 7:6; Phil 3:2).

Undeniably, it is the woman leading the conversation. Jesus keeps trying to shut down the conversation and the woman perseveres. She opens Jesus' eyes to a new perspective. Someone had to open Jesus' ministry in wider circles, beyond the statement, "I was sent only to the lost sheep of the house of Israel." (Matt 15:24) Earlier when Jesus sent out his disciples he urged them, "Go nowhere among the Gentiles, but go rather to the lost sheep of the house of Israel." (Matt 10:5b)

No one can doubt that Jesus first came to proclaim his message among the Jews. But somehow, somewhere, a broader mission began to emerge, a universal message intended for the whole world. Could it be the result of Jesus' conversation with two women: this Canaanite woman and the Samaritan woman at the well (John 4)? As a result of interacting with these two women, Jesus became comfortable when the Samaritans proclaimed, he is "truly the Savior of the world." (John 4:42) In both conversations, two spirited women led the way.

6 Read John 4:46–54—Another example is his response to the "royal official" who came to Cana to seek healing for his son back in Capernaum. Jesus' initial reaction was to complain, "Unless you (people) see signs and wonders you will not believe." (John 4:48) Yet when the royal official asked again, apparently his sincerity touched Jesus, for the child was healed at that moment. A royal official could have been a part of Herod's household, despised by the Jewish people. Jesus' initial reaction to the official was to

turn him away. "All you (people) want from me are signs and wonders—not genuine faith." But then he sensed this father's love for his son and his belief that Jesus could restore his son to fullness of health. It was a learning experience for Jesus and only then was Jesus able to respond with healing love.

It is important to recognize that the "you" in Greek is plural, therefore, describing a group or class of people rather than one royal official. Jesus moved from treating the man as a member of a social class, Herod's despised household, to treating the official as a loving and faithful father. Again, Jesus grew in his acceptance. His circle widened.

7 Read Luke 4:16-30—On Jesus' first visit back to Nazareth after the launch of his public ministry, things did not go well. So poorly, in fact, that Jesus couldn't return again to his hometown. They practically killed him for saying inflammatory statements about God's preferential treatment of two Gentiles. They were expecting a nationalistic savior not a savior of the world. I suspect Jesus learned something from that interaction and realized that as he approached other villages, a gentler touch was needed. In the midst of his conversation with his fellow Nazarenes, it suddenly occurred to Jesus, "Truly I tell you, no prophet is accepted in the prophet's hometown." (24) He surely wouldn't have returned to Nazareth in the first place had he realized their reaction. The comment by Jesus indicates that what he learned from his interaction with the Nazarenes guided him in future interactions. The statement, "no prophet is welcome in his hometown" reflects Jesus' admission that, like everyone else, he had to function within limits and boundaries. This admission was likely the basis of his later realizing the inevitability of his own death. He would not be able to win acceptance among Israel's faith leaders, just as he failed with the leaders of his own village.

8 Read Matthew 13:54-58 (Mark 6:1-6)—We can also see this in the way the Nazarenes knew Jesus before he left home. It is rather amazing that they did not know him as a miracle worker, filled with divine wisdom, or a teacher. He grew up among them and the Nazarenes had this to say upon his return: "Is not this Jesus, the son of Joseph, whose father and mother we know? How can he now say, 'I have come down from heaven?'" (John 6:42)

When he returned to Nazareth, they said, "Where did the man get this wisdom and these miraculous powers? This is the carpenter's son, surely?" "Is not his mother the woman called Mary? ..So where did the man get it all?" (Matt 13:54-56; Mark 6:1-6)

As he grew up among them, they hadn't noticed anything extraordinary about him. John reports, "Not even his brothers had faith in him." (7:5) The "Jesus" the Nazarenes knew as a child and the "Jesus" they were meeting

as an adult were nearly unrecognizable. He had experienced transformational learning from his time with John, from his baptism, from his days in
the wilderness. He was Jesus of Nazareth, in that he came from that village,
but he was Jesus-Beyond-Nazareth due to the intervening growth and understanding he had experienced.

Jesus experienced *metanoia* in the wilderness in his interaction with
John and his disciples. As such, he became the "Jesus-Beyond-Nazareth."

9 Read Luke 4:1–14—Another example of Jesus learning was his being
"sent" into the wilderness to be tested and tempted. "Then Jesus was led
up by the Spirit to be tempted by the devil." (Matt 4:1) It does not say: The
devil thought he could tempt Jesus, but was sadly mistaken. Jesus wasn't
play-acting: he was tempted three times in the wilderness. He could have
turned toward or away from God. The wilderness was used by God's Holy
Spirit to purify Jesus and prepare him for what stood ahead. He entered
the wilderness in one state of being and he departed in God's new place.
He learned from that experience. "Then Jesus, filled with the power of the
Spirit, returned to Galilee. . ." (Luke 4:14a) The Holy Spirit led Jesus into
the most daunting learning test of his young life. Jesus had to pass the test
before beginning his ministry. And only after he resisted these temptations,
was he able to return to Galilee ready to launch his ministry, (Luke 4:14)
"filled with the Holy Spirit."

10 John the Baptist was more proactive in teaching his disciples how
to pray. (Luke 11:1) It would have been impossible to create "The
Lord's Prayer" without deep introspection. The request, "Teach us to pray as
John taught his disciples," came to Jesus at the disciples' initiative. This suggests that Jesus might have been unaware of the extent to which his disciples
were struggling in their prayer life. The result was Jesus offering "The Lord's
Prayer" to his disciples. Often when we are challenged, as Jesus was by his
disciples, we find ourselves rising to unparalleled heights. This has become a
prayer repeated by millions of Christians in every part of the world. Would
he have offered this prayer had his disciples not requested it?

Jesus was praying "in a certain place," when his disciples came to him
asking him how to pray. Jesus was frequently criticized for his lack of austerity, for his partying and drinking, for his lack of fasting, and the lack of spiritual preparedness of his disciples. This is the only example of Jesus teaching
his disciples to pray—and it came, not at his instigation, but at their request.

Once he learned of their need, he responded.

11 Read John 7:1–14—It says that "Jesus did not wish to go about in Judea (but rather remain in Galilee) because the Jews (authorities) were looking for an opportunity to kill him." (1b) However, there must have been some uncertainty in his mind. His own brothers from Nazareth came to him and urged him to go to Judea for the Festival of Booths. "Show yourself to the world," they urged (4c). The Gospel of John explains, "(For not even his brothers believed in him.)" (5) But actually their words seem to suggest that they wanted him to expand his witness and have a larger impact than Galilee afforded. Later, Jesus changed his mind but instead went to Jerusalem "in secret." (10c) Even after arriving in secret, in "the middle of the festival Jesus went up into the temple and began to teach. The Jews (crowds) were astonished at it. . ." (14–15a) From conversation and interaction (how most of us learn), Jesus changed his position from staying away from Jerusalem, to entering in secret, to entering the temple and publicly teaching. This is a wonderful example of how his mind was changed by interaction with his brothers.

12 Read Matthew 16:13–17—While Jesus asked 79 "teaching questions" in the Gospel of Matthew, he also asked four questions as a learner. And two of them were highly significant. He asked his disciples, "Who do people say the Son of Man is?" (Matt 16:13) He wanted to know what the crowds were saying of him. It was not a rhetorical question. But his follow-up question was even more significant: "But who do you say that I am?" (15) And Peter's response led Jesus to affirm Peter for his spiritual insight. It was a learning conversation between Jesus and his closest disciples.

The passage clearly affirms that Jesus wasn't omniscient. He needed to know what his disciples had been hearing about him from others—comments the crowds would not share directly with Jesus.

13 Read Luke 2:41–51—As a boy, Jesus caused his parents "great anxiety" by not joining the Galilean entourage as they returned home from Jerusalem. He was fully engaged with the teachers in the temple. But traveling in the first-century was dangerous, which is why the Galileans traveled in a group. Roman soldiers would have loved to find a young Jewish boy hurrying to catch up with his family. What they would do to him would leave a life-long emotional scar. While it was wonderful to interact with scholars in the Temple, was it so wonderful to disobey or disregard his parents? Once Jesus realized the great anxiety he had caused his parents, he returned to Nazareth "and was obedient to them." (Lk 2:51b) The story is unmistakable in its message: Jesus wasn't yet ready to launch his ministry. He had a great deal more learning and preparation ahead of him.

14 Read Mark 3:20–35—We see Jesus learning through troubling parts of his relationship with his mother. The miracle at Cana was clearly not in his plans, but it was in hers (John 2). Later in his ministry, Mary came to Capernaum with his brothers and sisters to "restrain him" (3:21) and bring him home, after scholars from Jerusalem had come to her claiming that Jesus was filled with Beelzebul. Even people in his Capernaum crowd were saying, "He has gone out of his mind." (Mark 3:21) In this confrontational context, Jesus turned from his mother and siblings and instead embraced his followers as his true family. (Mark 3:22–35)

Yet, from the distance this episode likely created, the next time we see Mary was when she stood at the foot of the cross, watching Jesus die. She was in a very new place, a place of more profound faith.

The occasional tension in his relationship with his mother likely created learning opportunities for both of them.

15 Read Mark 11:12–14, 20–24—I think this passage could be called, "Making the Best from our Mistakes." Jesus was entering Jerusalem from Bethany, the day after Palm Sunday. And he was hungry. Jesus grew up in an agricultural setting and he would know the season for fig trees bearing fruit, just as we know that apples are in season in the Fall and other fruit trees in the mid to late summer. Jesus understood the cycle of the fig tree as he spoke of it in Mark 13:28. But we wouldn't walk up to an apple tree in April expecting to find a ripe apple. "Jesus went to see whether perhaps he would find anything on it" to eat. "When he came to it, he found nothing but leaves, for it was not the season for figs." (13b) Then Jesus cursed the tree as he said, "May no one ever eat fruit from you again." (14a)

The setting is important. Jesus was entering Jerusalem to do the most provocative act of his ministry: attacking the money-changers in the temple and driving them out. He was obviously filled with anxiety because this act would provoke the Jewish authorities like none other, sealing his fate. Why curse a fig tree, when the fig tree is performing just as God designed it to do? It was designed to grow green leaves out of season and figs in season. We might agree that cursing a fig tree for performing as God designed it was perhaps not Jesus' best day nor the high point in his ministry. There are very few destructive actions that Jesus took in his ministry. This is one, for seeming little purpose. Jesus tried to live a life of God's intention. When he didn't succeed, it was a learning opportunity.

By the next morning, the fig tree had withered "away to its roots." (20b) When the disciples walked by it and Peter noticed, Jesus then tried to add purpose to his hasty action from the day before. This time he spoke of the power of prayer. While it added purpose to his somewhat unnecessary action of the day before, it didn't fully redeem it.

16 Read Mark 11:15–19—In between the two instances of the fig tree story above, we read of another uncharacteristic action of Jesus. The money-changers were in the temple in order that those coming to bring their offerings to God could pay, not with an offensive Roman coin, but in a coin acceptable for the temple. And those selling doves were there to assist families bringing their children to be dedicated to God in the temple. So while there may have been excesses, these people were not disrespecting the temple. They were a vital part of people coming to the temple in obedience and faithfulness. What Jesus really accomplished in overturning the tables was to disrupt the vital economy of the temple and income of the ruling Jewish class. A significant amount of money was needed not only to keep the temple functioning but also to pay fine salaries to the aristocracy that ruled the temple. And on this day, Jesus disrupted the economic support of the temple and the livelihood of those who lived off these offerings. "He would not allow anyone to carry anything through the temple." (16) And when the chief priests and scribes heard of this, "they kept looking for a way to kill him. . ." (18b)

What Jesus did was edgy. And sometimes we are called to be confrontational. When I served as a pastor of a downtown church in Dayton, Ohio, the downtown at the time was quite vital with two large department stores and served as the headquarters of several multi-national corporations. There was a proposal to build a by-pass interstate highway around Dayton connecting the south to the east, and thereby bypassing downtown. I was in a group of concerned clergy who felt this would drain the city of its vitality. We tried to change the decision to build the highway out in the cornfields beyond the city. One day, in frustration, we decided to go out to the proposed bypass, where large earth-moving equipment was already at work, and, wearing liturgical robes and banners, we sat down in the middle of the track and at least for a few hours, we stopped their forward momentum. The bypass was built, of course, and it did drain the vitality from downtown and the inner city and the cornfields turned into the most pristine office complexes, universities and neighborhoods pulling the economic center away from the city and away from the poor. Do I typically stretch out in front of earth-moving equipment? No. I only did so after much consultation, prayer, and discernment.

Jesus' edgy action in the temple also required consultation with his disciples, prayer with his community, and communal discernment. I think his hastiness with the fig tree was a sign of his anxiousness over the larger action he was contemplating. It is a long way from the Beatitudes to the temple confrontation and one can only make such a journey with an open mind and heart. It was a learning journey for Jesus.

17 The Son of Man Prophecies.—The Son of Man Prophecies are repeated multiple times in the Synoptic Gospels. They are repeated five times in Matthew, four times in Mark, and four times in Luke (see footnote 36). We really don't know the reason the prophecy is repeated so many times but the fact that it is repeated in so many different forms in the Synoptic Gospels suggests that this is more than a literary technique by the three authors.

Four things are in common: this prophecy was shared only with Jesus' inner circle. Secondly, he did not share it until mid-way in the Gospels when he "turned his face" toward Jerusalem to initiate the final chapter of his earthly pilgrimage. Thirdly, the one event that precipitated Jesus sharing this prophecy is Peter's affirmation of Jesus as the Messiah. And finally, the disciples were woefully ill-prepared for this prophecy and argued against it when Jesus repeated it (Matt 16:22–23).

It is fair to assume that Jesus first shared the prophecy in its simplest form: "So the Son of Man is about to suffer at their hands." (Matt 17:12c) Or, "How then is it written about the Son of Man, that he is to go through many sufferings and be treated with contempt?" (Mark 9:12b) Or, "The Son of Man is going to be betrayed into human hands." (Luke 9:44) Or, the Son of Man "must first endure much suffering and be rejected by this generation." (Luke 17:24)

Why the simplest forms first? Because it doesn't seem humanly possible that Jesus could put into words the most complete versions of this prophecy until he had lived into it for some time and heard himself share it out-loud a few times. The simplest forms shared above are found in all three Synoptic Gospels. And in these three Gospels, the more complete forms are also found, such as, "See, we are going up to Jerusalem, and everything that is written about the Son of Man by the prophets will be accomplished. For he will be handed over to the Gentiles; and he will be mocked and insulted and spat upon. After they have flogged him, they will kill him, and on the third day he will rise again." (Luke 18: 31–33)

So this progression from a simple to a detailed form is recorded in all three Synoptic Gospels, though not necessarily listed in that order. When did Jesus learn his own destiny? The fact that he didn't share it with his disciples until well into his earthly ministry indicates that this is around the time when he was first able to articulate it. Once he had lived with the confrontation and the controversy surrounding his ministry, he then began to understand where this would lead. At that point he was open to the Holy Spirit teaching him about his painful destiny.

It is also important to note that it was Peter's declaration that Jesus was "the Messiah, God's Anointed," which precipitated this Son of Man prophecy. Often new realities coalesce in our minds when we hear them stated for the first time.

In my home church, the college students who were away at school led the Sunday evening worship service on the Sunday after Christmas. One of the junior or senior young men (of course!) was asked to preach the sermon. This was a long tradition. However, during Christmas vacation of my freshman year, there was no sophomore, junior or senior male available to preach. So, they asked me. Actually, I think they asked my mother while I was still at school. She was harder for me to respond in the negative!

So, as a freshman, I preached. At the close of the service, all of the college students were gathered up front and one of my mother's closest friends, Corinne Barbarick, came down the aisle. She couldn't get right up to me because it was crowded, so she used her booming voice to declare, "Steve, someday, you are going to be a preacher!" I was mortified. Everyone heard it. And it was the last thing I would have chosen for myself. But I also vividly remember Corinne articulating that vision, and, it took a few years, but it came to pass. I became a preacher. It could have happened without Corinne, but her spoken statement, while embarrassing at the time, pushed the reality along.

In like manner, I think Peter's declaration, heretofore in the Gospels not yet articulated, pushed the reality along. And the increasing confrontation and volatility of Jesus' interaction with the Jerusalem authorities also prompted Jesus to begin speaking resolutely of his destiny on earth.

I once surmised that Jesus repeated the prophecy so often because his disciples were slow to grasp its meaning. That is true. But I think Jesus repeating the prophecy, from simple form to complex, was also for the purpose of deepening his resolve. When we hear ourselves state things publicly, it may have the greater impact upon ourselves than others.

In several of the more complete versions of the Son of Man prophecy, it ends with "they will kill him, and on the third day he will rise again." He never elaborates or explains the third day prophecy. It is almost as if shared without joy or relief. He first has to go through hell before he can get there.

This represents one of the most significant awakenings of Jesus' life. He finally grasped his destiny.

18 Read Mark 14:32–42—We certainly recognize Jesus learning in Gethsemane, where he felt God's absence. In prayer in the garden,

"Jesus began to be distressed and agitated." (33) He said to his inner circle, "I am deeply grieved, even to death. . ." (34) In Luke, "his sweat became like great drops of blood falling down to the ground." (22:44) His honest request, "Take this cup from me," was as human a request as ever heard. And his "nevertheless" was as honest an admission of learning as ever heard. Jesus was caught up in his own fear and dread, and "nevertheless" represented a profound insight that caused him to make a dramatic mid-course correction on that crucial night. His heavy heart was finally ready to be obedient to God. His prayer gave him courage.

One thing to note about this prayer is that in the Gospel of Mark, Jesus began by saying, "Abba, Father. . ." Mark kept the Aramaic word, *Abba*, to underscore the authenticity of this prayer. This one certainly came from his lips!

Luke added, after Jesus asked to be relieved of this suffering, "Then an angel from heaven appeared to him and gave him strength. . ." (22:43) He lacked the strength, resolve, and courage necessary to do what God was asking of him. The angel gave him the strength to carry through. In Mark, Jesus came back to his disciples three times, clearly needing their solidarity, their prayers, and their support. And all three times they failed him and could not remain awake or attentive to his distress.

With the help of inspiration from heaven, Jesus mustered the courage to face the cross. But it was courage that was seriously lacking when he first entered Gethsemane.

19 Upon the cross, when he cried out with a loud voice, "My God, my God, why have you forsaken me?" (Matt 27:46), he felt as far from God as humanly possible. In Mark and Matthew, this prayer is quoted directly from the Hebrew (Psalm 22:2) and only then translated for non-Hebrew-speaking readers. These are Jesus' genuine words of anguish, in the language he knew. From utter despair in that moment, he opened his heart and surely died in the arms of his Heavenly Father. It was Jesus' final moment of learning to surrender to God's Great Design. He was learning even upon the cross.

20 Read John 6:14–15—After Jesus had fed the 5,000, beginning with the contribution of the small lad with his loaves and fishes, many in the crowd reached this conclusion: "When the people saw the sign that he had done, they began to say, 'This is indeed the prophet who is to come into the world.'" The story continues, "*When Jesus realized* that they were about to come and take him by force to make him king, he withdrew again to the mountain by himself." Watching the responses of the crowd, and learning of their intentions, Jesus reached the conclusion he should withdraw before things got out of hand.

Learning at its best comes from interaction with others, particularly as we become aware of their motivation. Withdrawing to a lonely place was his opportunity to ponder what had just occurred and why the crowd had reacted in this way. They were about to "take him by force." Was there something he could have said or done to have brought about a different outcome? Time and distance gave him opportunity for personal reflection.

21 Read Mark 13:32—Jesus lived in an apocalyptic era of great expectation for how God would bring human history to a close and introduce a new era of divine reign. And he was teaching about this one day in Mark's Gospel. But then he said, "But about that day or hour no one knows, neither the angels in heaven, nor the Son, but only the Father." Jesus acknowledged that while he had keen insight to teach about God's coming reign, there were limits to his knowledge: "Only God knows." He was not omniscient.

22 Read Mark 8:22–26—In Bethsaida, people brought a blind man and begged Jesus to heal him. He led the blind man out of the village, put saliva on his eyes, laid his hands on him and asked, "Can you see anything?" The man looked up and said, "I can see people, but they look like trees walking." Jesus' healing was only partial, but not complete. It required Jesus to lay his hands on the man a second time before he could fully see things clearly.

Why is this incident reported in the Gospel? Does it not suggest that Jesus learned something that day about God's healing power? Looking ahead two chapters, to Mark 10:46–52, we find Jesus in Jericho with another blind man and this time Jesus was able to heal the blind man with only one attempt. "Immediately the blind man regained his sight. . ." (10:52b)

23 Read Matthew 10:5—When Jesus first sent out his disciples, he told them, ". . .enter no town of the Samaritans." Yet, we learn from several later occasions when Jesus purposefully entered Samaritan areas and villages. In John's Gospel, as Jesus was traveling from Judea to Galilee, instead of following the customary journey of walking into the wilderness around Samaria so as to avoid contact, Jesus "had to go through Samaria." (4:4) Jesus was crossing a Jewish boundary, for all Jews of his day were taught to avoid contact with Samaritans. Both groups held severe contempt of the other. Something changed with Jesus. He began by directing his disciples to avoid Samaritans, and then led them into Samaria, surprising his disciples by the depth of which he interacted with a Samaritan woman, breaking all social convention.

24 Compare Jesus and James. James was Jesus' next oldest brother. They grew up in the same village and in the same family. No early church leader knew Jesus for longer than James. These two eldest brothers must have shared many experiences in their first 25 years together in the small village of Nazareth. If Joseph died early, as suspected, then leadership of the family first fell to Jesus, and then to James. And if Jesus was to be free to leave his family in pursuit of his public ministry, then James had to be ready to take over the mantle of leadership for the family and be a support to his mother and his siblings. Since carpentry was the family business, James surely had to be ready to be a carpenter like Joseph and Jesus.

There is no evidence that James followed Jesus around Galilee associated with his ministry. Indeed, there are times when "Jesus' brothers" stand in opposition to him.

"James, who is identified as 'the Lord's brother' (Gal 1:19), a 'pillar' of the Jerusalem Church (Gal 2:9), a participant in the conference(s) at Jerusalem (Gal 2:1–10; Acts 15:1–20), and as one who experienced the risen Lord (I Cor 15:2)."[21]

James, as leader of the Jerusalem church, held a more conservative view toward the inclusion of Gentiles among the followers of Jesus. Jesus also began from the same strict, conservative stance where James continued. But Jesus' ministry and interaction broadened his world-view. His experiences led him to reach out and include Samaritans and Gentiles, tax collectors, women and sinners. Jesus' ministry erased those dividing walls. James' world was more exclusive, centered first in Nazareth and then as leader of the Jerusalem church. You can hear a young Jesus and his brother, James, identifying with the saying, "I was sent only to the lost sheep of the House of Israel." (Matt 25:24) James stayed in this comfortable place. But Jesus moved out to more uncomfortable places and people groups. James reflects Jesus' roots, his heritage. You can almost hear James' discomfort with Jesus arriving back in their home town proclaiming God's preferential treatment of Gentiles. He himself had to have been shocked.

At the Jerusalem conference, James attempted to mediate between the controversial sides of this dispute. But later, Paul claimed that James attempted to place restrictions upon Gentile Christians in Antioch:

". . .while the Acts 15 conference reflects a minimal imposition of the Jewish law on the gentile Christians by James, his authority as felt in the

---

21. *Anchor Bible Dictionary, Vol. 3,* 620.

Antiochian dispute (Gal 2:11–14) conveys a strictness on his part concerning Jewish Christian observance of the Law."[22]

James later advised Paul to participate in a temple ceremony (Acts 21:18–24) to prove his allegiance to the Law. James tended to be more traditional than Jesus or Paul.

In James' interaction with Paul, we can recognize Jesus' Jewish beginnings, a more narrow view of the world. It shows how far Jesus traveled by the end of his ministry.

25 Consider this question: How did Jesus learn to overcome the stereotypes and biases of his day?

Was Jesus, as a child, taught to stereotype tax collectors as sinners?

Was Jesus, as a child, exposed to the idea that Gentiles were inferior? Would he have heard them referred to as dogs?

Was young Jesus taught that women were not equal to men?

Was Jesus, as a child, taught to despise Samaritans?

Did Jesus, as a Galilean, learn stereotypes about Judean Jews?

Was Jesus raised to fear lepers—and stay clear of them?

Was Jesus taught to marginalize eunuchs?

Was he taught that women deserve the blame and burden of divorce and adultery?

Was he taught to hate the Romans?

There is no way that he could have been raised in his culture in the first century without being exposed to all of these stereotypes. He grew up in a Galilean culture steeped in these biases. No matter how remarkable were his parents, it wasn't possible.

Bishop John A.T. Robinson, wrote, "Jesus evidently starts with all the inbuilt racial prejudices of the Jew, describing the Gentiles as dogs. Indeed, he could not have been what it meant to be a Jew of the first century without a whole complex of national memories, repressions and alienations. He reacts instinctively, as I believe he does in the similar story in the Fourth Gospel (John 4:46—54), where the court official who seeks help for his sick boy is dismissed with the categorizing plural, 'Oh, you people, all you want to see is signs and wonders'—for the man was a representative of Herod's house, the half-breed quisling king. But in each case the greatness and goodness of Jesus lay not in his being exempt from these distorting limitations but in his power, shown also in his attitude to the Samaritans, to break through and come out on the other side of them. As a result of such experiences he emerged a different and bigger man."[23]

22. *Anchor Bible Dictionary, Vol. 3,* 620.

23. Robinson, *The Human Face of God,* 85.

We can ask the above questions in reverse:

Did Jesus, as a child or teenager, ever eat in the home of a tax collector or socialize with them?

Did he hang out as a child or teenager with prostitutes and known sinners?

Did he as a young person befriend a eunuch?

Did he hang out with the unrighteous?

Did he ever walk through Samaria with his parents?

Did he play with Gentile children or children of sinners?

It would have been impossible for any of these things to occur. The cultural doors were closed. It was only as he matured that he learned the importance of crossing boundaries in radical ways. His parents, like all righteous Jews, would have kept the child Jesus well within the boundaries of righteous living.

Who taught Jesus not to treat Samaritans as inferior? Did the woman at the well help him view Samaritans in a new light? Don't you think that Jesus had to meet a eunuch at some point to reach the conclusion that they could be part of the kingdom of God? Did Zacchaeus change the way Jesus viewed tax collectors?

Learning often involves un-learning. We earlier reach conclusions and form assumptions that no longer fit our expanding experiences. And we have to un-learn by setting aside those conclusions and assumptions to consider other alternatives. There was a recent article in the Washington Post reporting that Nebraska has resettled more refugees per capita than any other state. Lutheran Family Services of Nebraska has settled 1,531 refugees, including 21 Syrian families. One resident of Omaha stated that after 9/11 he hated Muslims. After some Syrian families moved into his neighborhood, he said, "The Muslims here were all about family, and they just loved everyone. . . These people, they really changed my heart."[24]

Another example is the rapidly changing perspectives in our society related to homosexuality and gay marriage. Rarely has change occurred so quickly. Not assuming everyone has reached the same conclusion, but it would be very hard to be in American society for the last twenty years and not have re-thought your earlier convictions.

Another example would be connectivity. Due to technological advances not even imagined thirty years ago, consider how our world has changed due to instant global connectivity. How much has it changed our understanding by carrying around in the palm of our hands tools that connect us to knowledge about nearly everything? I was in the basement of my parent's

24. *Christian Century Magazine, March 15, 2017, quoting The Washington Post, 9.*

home a few years ago and came across a set of the *Encyclopedia Britannica* that I had used many times as a child. It was yellowed, moldy, brittle and stained. I now have everything in that encyclopedia available through my cell phone. We have had to learn to embrace technology, when first many resisted it. I recall when on-line dating sites began, I was opposed. I felt it turned what should have been natural human relationships into unnatural on-line vetting. I have since known many couples who have met on these on-line services which provided wonderful opportunities for relationships to unfold. I learned what technology can do.

I co-pastor with a young woman from Haiti. While growing up in that island nation, there was no possibility that a woman could serve as a pastor of a Baptist church. So, she didn't even entertain such a notion. It was unthinkable. However, that situation is changing in the United States and now I co-pastor with a Haitian woman with the full idea that someday she could pastor this church without me.

Jesus couldn't have been insulated from or impervious to others. That does not describe our Lord and Savior. He was open to others—he learned from them and with them. He surely learned bias as a child that required he unlearn later in life. Surely this was the work of the Holy Spirit in Jesus' life.

Question: How have you changed, your attitudes and biases,
over the years? How did it happen?

Jesus Journeyed

In the same chapter of Luke, the author tells us in straight-forward terms that Jesus grew, that he journeyed, that he was a learner:

> *"And as the child grew to maturity, he was filled with wisdom, and God's favour was with him." Luke 2:40 NJB*
> *"And as Jesus continued to grow in body and mind, he grew also in the love of God and of those who knew him." Luke 2:52 Phillips Modern English*

The real question becomes: how did Jesus get from "here" to "there"? This is what was remarkable about Jesus, not that he was already "there," but that he journeyed so incredibly well and so wondrously far. Isn't it also true for us? Most of us have journeyed some distance, traveling away from the biases, prejudices, and boundaries of our childhood to embrace something more sophisticated, more nuanced, and more perceptive as life progresses.

Jesus journeyed. He didn't stay where he began. Isn't that the point of the temptations of Jesus occurring just after his baptism? His baptism wasn't a celebration that Jesus had arrived but a recognition that he had begun! He was tempted in the wilderness. He needed to be tested. It wasn't easy for him—forty days of temptation! He yielded and let God lead him—out of the wilderness. And he had to get there the hard way, the human way, just like we learn. It's called the School of Hard Knocks. We learn by trial and error. We learn by misjudgments. We learn by overcoming bias taught to us when we were young.

I have certainly learned through the "school of hard knocks." One of my first ministry positions was as a youth minister in a church in my college town. The young woman who was president of the Methodist youth was very thoughtful for her age and also happened to be the mayor's daughter. She was around 16 years old and I was around 18 years old. And we spent a lot of time together planning upcoming youth activities.

Toward the end of that year, I decided to ask her out on a date. I will never forget walking up to her front door, when her father, the mayor, opened the door. He greeted me skeptically as I suspect it was his daughter's first date. We had no more than walked down the sidewalk before I realized that I had made a mistake. My relationship with this young woman changed almost instantly. I was no longer her pastor; now, I was her date. Mixing roles, the evening felt awkward. And the next youth group meeting was entirely different. I was now just another guy, checking out the girls and every guy and girl knew it. This delivered a fatal blow to my ministry. Things were never the same. I learned the importance of appropriate boundaries.

I did not grow up around Jews in my small town in the Ozarks. And when I went away to college, I repeated a phrase I had often heard as a child without reflection on what it meant. I was in a conversation in which someone had negotiated skillfully for a better price and I said, "You really 'jewed' him down, didn't you?" One of those in the conversation took me aside to point out the blatant stereotyping involved with that expression. I remember feeling very embarrassed because I had no such intention.

The teenagers in my small town in the Ozarks knew about gay men. We teased each other with effeminate gestures and language. I wasn't athletic growing up and I was frightened that someone might think I was gay. Today, I have journeyed far from that fear and stereotyping. It was a stereotype that unfortunately stood in the way of developing vulnerable friendships with other men.

Question: How have you learned by trial and error?
Have you attended the School of Hard Knocks?

Jesus was known for his broadmindedness in crossing boundaries. The Pharisees recognized that Jesus "showed deference to no one. 'For you do not regard people with partiality.'" (Matt 22:16) In a society filled with judgments of others, Jesus had to learn an alternative way, and he was recognized for this. Do we really believe that:

- Jesus had no conversion experiences?

- He never felt a need to turn toward God?

- Jesus never needed to surrender to God's will?

- His baptism had no real meaning to him?

- Jesus never discovered God's call—because he already inherently knew it?

- He never felt God's absence or abandonment?

- Jesus never chose God in conscious deliberate decisions?

- His faith required no difficult decision-making and no cost?

- Jesus was never surprised by God?

- Struggle was alien to Jesus' life?

- Jesus had nothing to learn in life?

Jesus' life was full of struggle, of mystery, and of discovery. Like the rest of us, when he heard God whispering in his soul, it took him by surprise, and turned his world upside down. Is this not the meaning of his wilderness temptations? Emilie Griffin describes the beautiful experience of "Turning" with these stunning words:

"When I first began to experience the power of God in my own life, I could hardly believe it. Something very real and discernible was happening to me, yet I felt it could not or should not be happening. God was speaking to me; God was calling me. He spoke no louder than a whisper, but I heard him. And each time that I heard him, and chose him, a change occurred, the opening of a door I had not guessed was there."[25]

Prayer Is Learning

As all who fervently believe in prayer, Jesus turned to prayer to receive from a Power greater than himself. Prayer is reverencing God as folded hands suggest, but prayer is also receiving from God as open palms suggest. There

25. Griffin, *Turning, Reflections on the Experience of Conversion,* 15.

would have been no need for Jesus to pray if he already knew everything God knew or if he already possessed God's full insight. He prayed, as we all do, to learn and receive from God. Henri Nouwen states, "Praying. . .means being constantly ready to let go of your certainty and to move on further than where you are now."[26]

There is something calming and reassuring as we "talk with God," sharing our needs and concerns. But prayer matters little if that is all it is. Through prayer, we must place ourselves in a receiving position. As learners, we enter into the posture of prayer through silence, reflection, contemplation, meditation, and discernment to listen for God's unique Word for us. God's Word is never what we dictate to God and often what we least expect. It is sometimes a reassuring word but as often a transforming word. Prayer leaves us in the position of a learner—to receive all that we can—to stand ready before God—to be open to God's leadership. The Prophet Isaiah testified to this, "And when you turn to the right or when you turn to the left, your ears shall hear a word behind you, saying, 'This is the way; walk in it.'" (Isa 30:21)

On nine occasions in the three synoptic Gospels, Jesus engaged in a public act of prayer.[27] On eight occasions in those Gospels, he engaged in solitary prayer.[28] He maintained an active prayer life, seeking to be in tune with his Heavenly Father. The Lord's Prayer is a prayer rich with learning invocations. Particularly in solitary prayer, Jesus engaged in prayer in order to learn and receive:

- When he was baptized, (Luke 3:21), he was praying and through prayer received the vision and affirmation of the descending dove.

- Jesus devoted an all-night season of prayer before choosing and calling the Twelve (Luke 6:12).

- Upon hearing of the death of John the Baptist, (Matt 14:13) Jesus went off to pray in order to regain his balance and to absorb what this tragedy meant to him.

- Jesus was praying alone just before his disciples asked him to teach them how to pray. From that time of personal devotion, he offered the Lord's Prayer (Luke 11:1).

---

26. Nouwen, *With Open Hands,* 81.

27. Matt 15:36; Matt 19:13 (Luke 9:36; Mark 10:16); Matt 26:26; Matt 26:36; Luke 24:30; Luke 24:50–51; Matt 11:25; Luke 9:28; Luke 10:21.

28. Luke 23:46 (Matt 27:46); Luke 3:21; Matt 14:13; Luke 6:12; Luke 9:18; Mark 1:35; Mark 6:46 (Matt 14:23); Luke 11:1.

- Once when Jesus prayed, it opened his mind to ask questions of his disciples, to hear what the crowds were saying of him (Luke 9:18).

- He prayed on the cross (Luke 23:46; Matt 27:46), from which he drew strength to forgive and gain insight to see God at work through his dying.

Is prayer based upon a premise of learning?

Jesus urged his disciples to pray for courage, for insight, for illumination. In a statement that must have reflected Jesus' passion for solitary prayer, he once said, "What I say to you in the dark, tell in the light; and what you hear whispered, proclaim from the housetops." (Matt 10:27) "In the dark" are those times when we enter into Divine Mystery through prayer in order to discern how God is speaking to us.

Prayer involves, yes, even requires openness to learning. It is not only a devotional or pietistic practice. Prayer not only reinforces what is already known: it transforms us. If you believe in prayers for healing, then you believe prayer unleashes transformative power. Prayer changes things!

The Lost Years

We often speak of the "lost years" of Jesus' life—from his birth, to his Temple presentation at twelve to the launch of his ministry around the age of thirty. That's almost thirty years out of Jesus' thirty-three years that are lost to us. But what if no one had written the Gospels? If we were only Pauline Christians, nearly all of his years would be lost to us—save the events at the end of Jesus' life.

In modern times, we have discovered ancient written Gospels not previously known. There is an *Infancy Gospel of Thomas*[29] that relates miraculous deeds by the child Jesus. At five years old, Jesus was playing in a rushing stream. He took soft clay and formed twelve sparrows which later took flight. When he was five or six, Jesus commanded one child to die, and brought another child back to life. One day, his water jug broke when he was fetching water for his mother, and the child Jesus spread out his cloak, filled it with water and brought it to his mother. In his father's woodshop, he stretched a piece of wood to fit his father's specifications. One school teacher tried to teach Jesus and Jesus cursed the teacher who fell dead. This fanciful Gospel, written by someone as early as the second century, but no

29. Ehrman, translator; *The Infancy Gospel of Thomas*, 58–62.

later than the fifth century, paints a picture of a child capable of magic and miracles. He also laughed at others' misfortunes and punished those who challenged him.

For our purposes, multiple times in this Infancy Gospel there are teachers who try to take Jesus as a pupil. With one teacher he refused to recite the letters of the Greek alphabet (!) but when the teacher gave up, he recited them perfectly. Then, Jesus instructed the teacher and the teacher left shamed. Another teacher tried to teach young Jesus and Jesus' knowledge far surpassed his own and the teacher told Joseph, "You delivered a teacher to me, not a learner."

In this infancy Gospel, Jesus wasn't capable of learning because he was omniscient and omnipotent. In other words, he wasn't a human child at all but a divine being already embodying his life's mission. Clearly the canonical Gospels do not present him this way.

The Infancy Gospel of Thomas re-tells the story of Jesus going to Jerusalem with his parents at the age of twelve and staying behind with the Temple elders. It is told in nearly parallel fashion to Luke except that he "explained the main points of the law and riddles and the parables of the prophets" to the elders. (15:2) In the Gospel of Luke, Mary and Joseph found Jesus "sitting among the teachers, listening to them and asking them questions. And all who heard him were amazed at his understanding and his answers." (2:46b-47) In other words, Luke describes a young boy who asked questions, listened, and conversed with the elders: a learner. He exhibited a level of understanding unusual for his age, but not miraculous.

Jesus started out in this world as a defenseless baby in need of nurture. A godly being could have stood in his cradle and sent legions of angels to protect the male babies in Bethlehem from an approaching slaughter. Jesus needed his parents to flee in the night to Egypt where he could be protected from Herod's wrath.

If crowds of Galileans were lined up outside the humble childhood home of six-year-old Jesus, wanting to touch him and be healed of illness, wanting to hear his every utterance of God's wisdom, then surely the Gospels would have begun his ministry at the age of six, not thirty! They are silent about those years because they were years of preparation and learning by young Jesus, readying himself for God's destiny.

We can surmise that the Gospel writers did not view his teen and young adult years as noteworthy compared to his public ministry years. Jesus grew in stature and wisdom and maturity. He grew to the point where the light within his soul turned on and his public ministry began.

Do you believe in an "Arrived Jesus" or a "Becoming Jesus"?

Jesus' Healing Ministry and Miracles

Jesus' healing ministry and his frequent use of miracles might convince us that he had already "arrived" when he began his ministry. The fact that Jesus had healing powers is similar to the authority by which he spoke and acted. He was a Spirit-led person and teacher. Did he have to learn to open his heart and soul to the Spirit's leadership? Absolutely. Miracles are a work of faith, not magic. It's spiritual interaction, not dramatic performance.

The miracle at Cana was Jesus' first miracle in the Gospel of John and it showed some confusion between Jesus and his mother over the proper timing and use of his miracles. This was one exceptional instance when Jesus' miracle-working wasn't used to restore health to an individual. In this case, it was to change water to wine at a wedding so as to avoid embarrassment to the wedding party. This mattered greatly to Mary, but not so much to Jesus. "When the wine gave out, the mother of Jesus said to him, 'They have no wine.' And Jesus said to her, 'Woman, what concern is that to you and to me? My hour has not yet come.'" (John 2:3–4) Mary pushed ahead, nearly forcing Jesus to act against his will. If Mary and Jesus didn't yet agree on the role of miracles in his ministry, it might be safe to say that both were in a learning mode.

One time at Bethsaida, people brought a blind man to Jesus and begged him to touch him. Jesus led the man out of the village and ". . .when he had put saliva on his eyes and laid his hands on him, Jesus asked him, 'Can you see anything?' And the man looked up and said, 'I can see people, but they look like trees, walking.' Then Jesus laid his hands on his eyes again; and Jesus looked intently and his sight was restored, and he saw everything clearly." (Mark 8:22–25)

Here, Jesus' healing required two attempts. One might ask: Why does Mark include a story in which Jesus' first healing wasn't a complete success? Why not omit that story? This is Jesus' first healing of a blind person in Mark's Gospel. Clearly, Jesus was not summoning magical powers when he healed. He was summoning the power of God's Holy Spirit to work through him. And it is entirely possible, in this first healing of blindness, that Jesus faced a learning curve. Perhaps he needed to be more in tune with the spiritual power that was within him and the depth of God's spiritual power available to him.

A third example is in the raising of Lazarus from the dead. The story in John 11 suggests that Jesus didn't know the conclusion until it unfolded. Jesus reached Bethany late, after earlier learning that his friend Lazarus was dying. "When Jesus saw Mary weeping, and the Jews who came with her also weeping, he was greatly disturbed in spirit and deeply moved." (John 11:33)

Lazarus had been dead four days. Jesus entered into the pathos of his friends. "Jesus began to weep." (35) Why weep if you already know a positive conclusion? When Jesus came to Lazarus' tomb, he was "again greatly disturbed." (38) Jesus then prayed giving thanks for the way in which God has heard his prayers "always." (42) After his prayer the outcome became known, that indeed, Lazarus would be raised from the dead on that day. Otherwise, Jesus weeping and distress at the death of his friend made no sense. Jesus came to Bethany affirming the belief in the resurrection of the dead (23). But raising Lazarus from the dead on that day was the amazing outcome.

Jesus rarely put the emphasis on the act of healing, but more upon the act of faith behind the healing. When he healed the woman who had been hemorrhaging, she touched him in a crowd and the healing was anonymous. But that wasn't enough for Jesus. He stopped the procession and asked, "Who touched me?" When the frightened woman came forward, Jesus celebrated her depth of faith. Jesus became upset when people came to him and all they wanted was signs and miracles. He had little patience with this. It wasn't his intent to put on a Traveling Healing Show. He wanted to connect with people in a deeply spiritual way, connecting his faith and theirs.

It doesn't detract in any way from these connections to say that the power and authority that Jesus used came as a gift to him, and he had to learn how best to use these gifts. "And the power of the Lord was with him to heal." (Luke 5:17c)

Biblical Perfection

What about the doctrinal notion that Jesus was perfect? We need to unpack the original meaning of the biblical concept translated as *perfect*. The Greek word is *teleios*. It means fulfillment, wholeness, completeness or destiny. It appears nineteen times in the New Testament. It often meant the fulfillment of the goal that God has set out for us. Jesus perfectly realized God's calling in his life. But our modern understanding of perfection, without blemish, without sin, or without mistake, is not the biblical meaning of *teleios*.

Jesus answered Herod Antipas, "Listen, I am casting out demons and performing cures today and tomorrow, and on the third day *I finish my work*." (Luke 13:32 NRSV; "I reach my goal," REB; "I accomplish my purpose," NAB; "I attain my end." NJB) The word is *teleios*, and it literally means "on the third day I am being made perfect." In Hebrews, the author refers on three occasions to Jesus being made perfect through his suffering. "Although he was a Son, he *learned obedience* through what he suffered; and having been made perfect, *he became* the source of eternal salvation for all who obey him. . ." (Hebrews 5:8–9) Hebrews also reports that "God. . .made the pioneer of (our) salvation perfect through suffering." (2:10) To be made "perfect through suffering" is an entirely different meaning of the word than our modern use. Through his willingness to suffer and die, Jesus was "made perfect" by God to realize his incarnational destiny.

The Bible doesn't claim that Jesus had already "arrived" when he came into this world. It describes a human being with God's claim on his life, even before he was born. But Jesus had to grow into that calling. He arrived in one place and had to journey to God's place—from "here" to "there." And that is what was remarkable about his life.

Bishop John A.T. Robinson wrote, "It has tended to be taken as axiomatic in Christian thinking and devotion that Jesus was complete and perfect in every respect. He must have had everything, he must have been everything—or he could not have been the Christ. And this has been a powerful influence in the separation of him from ordinary humanity. He has been set on a pedestal by himself, an immaculate paragon, of whom it was impossible to think that he should fall short in anything. And as such he quickly becomes unique not because he is normal but because he is abnormal. What we want to say of him as *the* man paradoxically undercuts his humanity. And this is a powerful factor today in making him for many an unreal figure with the static perfection of flawless porcelain, rather than a man of flesh and blood."[30]

It wasn't Jesus' perfection that amazed the crowds. No one said, "You are so perfect, so flawless." Rather, people recognized that unlike their teachers, "Jesus taught as one having authority." (Matt 7:29; also 21:23–24)

The modern idea of perfection is extremely harmful. Many people are perfectionists and their lives are miserable trying to chase after an impossible standard. Many people are forced to deny their mistakes or flaws as they maintain a facade of perfectionism. Many others loathe themselves because of their flaws. Wouldn't we be better off if we accepted the biblical definition of perfection? What if instead we sought wholeness, we sought to complete our inner destinies, we sought fulfillment? Sure, we'll make mistakes along the way, but that isn't the point. We're headed in the right direction, seeking God's gift of fulfillment with our whole hearts. That's the biblical idea of perfection, which Jesus perfectly embodied.

How does the modern idea of perfection adversely affect you, or the people you love?

---

30. Robinson, *The Human Face of God*, 68.

In the gospel hymn, *"All the Way My Savior Leads Me,"* I am drawn to the first stanza which seems to state this well:

> *"All the way my Savior leads me, what have I to ask beside?*
> *Can I doubt his tender mercy who through life has been my guide?*
> *Heavenly peace, divinest comfort, here by faith in him to dwell,*
> *For I know, what-e'er befall me, Jesus doeth all things well."*
> Fanny J. Crosby, 1875

Jesus doeth all things well. He offers me comfort, peace, and hope. He "doeth all things well." This is the biblical understanding of perfection.

Was Jesus a Sinner?

After one respected layperson heard these ideas in a series of lectures, he said, "I'm glad you didn't raise the question of Jesus sinning. That question should be 'off the table.'" I understand the caution which this question raises; indeed, I feel it in my soul as well.

There is a way to answer this admittedly perplexing question that is clear and irrefutable. The Jews of the first century divided the world between the Righteous and Sinners. Gentiles were sinners. And so were non-observant Jews. Jews who took their covenantal relationship with God seriously and sought to be faithful to God's commandments were righteous. Those who ignored this were sinners. There is no question that Jesus was not a sinner, but a righteous Jew throughout his lifetime.

However, this does not mean that a righteous Jew could not commit a sin. Look at the circle of condemning righteous men who were about to stone a woman caught in adultery. Jesus said to them, "Let anyone among you who is without sin be the first to throw a stone at her." (John 8:7) And one by one they dropped their stones because these righteous men were keenly aware that each had sinned.

Jesus was cautious regarding extreme claims about himself, as was evident in his response to the rich young ruler, "...who ran up and knelt before Jesus and asked him, 'Good Teacher, what must I do to inherit eternal life?' Jesus first set aside his question and said to him, 'Why do you call me good? No one is good but God alone.'" (Mark 10:17—18) Jesus was uncomfortable with the young man calling him "good," reserving that attribute for God alone.

Did Jesus ever commit a sin? This is a difficult and awkward question for most Christians and we might respond, "Of course not." We may prefer to not even ask this question. Yet, what about his not informing his parents that he was staying behind in Jerusalem when he was twelve years old? Was this a sin? It could be viewed that way. Does sin require a conscious decision to do wrong? Is not considering the feelings of one's parent a sin? Is ignoring the instructions of one's parents a sin?

Can we hold a twelve-year-old child to a standard of sinlessness? Can we hold twelve-year-old Jesus to the same moral standard as Jesus in the final season of his life when he courageously challenged the Jerusalem status quo?

Paul had interesting responses to this question as to whether Jesus sinned. In 2 Cor 5:21, Paul wrote, "For our sake God made him to be sin who knew no sin. . ." (Revised English Bible: ". . .God made him one with human sinfulness.") When Paul said "who knew no sin" he was referring to the pre-existent Christ who was with God before his birth. Then, he was born into the human situation. "Made him to be sin" suggests that Jesus became like us. And in 2 Cor 5:16, Paul wrote, ". . .we once knew Christ from a human point of view (but) we know him no longer in this way." "We once knew Christ from a human point of view" suggests that at an earlier point in his life we could regard him as fully human, but that "we no longer know him (the Resurrected Lord) this way."

In these two passages in 2 Corinthians, Paul argues that before he entered the world, Jesus knew no sin. And then he entered a sinful world. Then Paul argues that Jesus was released from this sinful world through the power of the resurrection and we can no longer regard him in the same way.

Even Jesus' unique term for himself, "the Son of Man," which no one else in the Gospels used, suggested that he viewed himself as a son of humanity (which is what the expression literally means). "Son of God" suggests the opposite.

I think that once Jesus set his sight on Jerusalem, once he accepted the terrifying outcome of his life, I think he *perfectly and fully realized God's destiny for his life.* By that time, *he knew no sin,* and with Paul I believe "we can no longer know him this way."

Jesus was "fully human, fully divine." He came to understand his role as the Son of Man, representing all of humanity before God. That is the horizontal role. And he came to understand his role as the Son of God, standing in God's place for all humanity. That is the vertical role, and, like Paul, we understand that this came together on the cross.

Did Jesus make mistakes? If not, then he never learned from a mistake and he cannot be a model for us because we learn, most frequently, from our mistakes. How else can we view Jesus' interaction with the Syrophoenician woman except that he began in the wrong place and ended in the right place? (Mark 7:25–30) How else can we view Jesus in the Garden of

Gethsemane but that fear consumed him as he prayed and faith propelled him beyond the garden? How else can we view Jesus' cry of abandonment from the cross, before a deeper reservoir of faith took over and led him to die with courage? Jesus was on a journey and he was capable of learning from mistakes. Every chapter we know of Jesus' life suggests an amazing ability to learn and seek God's will. Paul's belief in Jesus' journey ("made him to be sin"; and "we once regarded him") points in the right direction.

Did Jesus die an innocent man? Absolutely. The "crimes" of which he was accused were false. He was put to death for no crime, no sin, and no mistake. He threatened the tenuous status quo of the Jewish Sanhedrin in Jerusalem. He criticized the serious compromises they made with the Romans in order to stay in power. And because he was a threat to stability, he was put to death. And he died an innocent man.

The author of Hebrews states that Jesus "learned obedience" (5:8), that he was "made perfect through suffering," (2:10). Author Joan Chittister states, "The great secret of life is how to survive struggle without succumbing to it, how to bear struggle without being defeated by it, how to come out of great struggle better than when we found ourselves in the midst of it. A spirituality of struggle exposes the secret to the world."[31] Jesus learned obedience through suffering and struggle. It's the same for each of us.

Bishop Robinson argues, ". . .for the biblical writers, while Jesus is totally human and therefore as independent of God as any other man, his whole life—and all that leads up to it and flows from it—is seen as the climax and fulfilment of a divine process going back to the beginning. His entire being is shaped and constituted by the destiny to be God's true man, the Son of his love, the very reflection and image of his person."[32]

Can you possibly be a learner if you cannot learn from your mistakes?

Nothing more needs to be said. Jesus overcame sin to stand as God's Representative to us, a mirror of God to us, and as our Representative before God. Jesus knew no sin as he became the Incarnation of God.

Marcus Borg writes, ". . .the decisive revelation of God is a *person*. . . Importantly, Jesus is not the revelation of 'all' of God, but of what can be seen of God in a human life. Some of God's traditional attributes or qualities cannot be seen in a human life. The omnipresence of God cannot be seen in a human life—a human being cannot be present everywhere. The infinity of God cannot be seen in a human life—a human being is by definition

31. Chittister, *Scarred by Struggle, Transformed by Hope*, 13.
32. Robinson, *The Human Face of God*, 201.

finite. So also the omnipotence: a human being cannot be all-powerful and still be human. So also omniscience: what could it mean to say that a human is 'omniscient' and that Jesus in particular was? That he would 'know everything'—including, for example, the theory of relativity and the capital of Oregon?

"So there is much of God that cannot be seen in a human life. But—and this is what matters—what can be seen is the character and passion of God. . . This is what Jesus reveals: the character and passion, the nature and will, of God."[33]

The Real Point of Jesus and Sin

The important thing about Jesus and sin is what his life, death, and resurrection accomplished. That is what matters. Jesus was all about tearing down the rigid dividing wall between the righteous and sinners in his first-century homeland. He mostly hung out with sinners on the "wrong side" of the wall: with tax collectors, with Samaritans, with lepers and those considered unclean, and with prostitutes. Even blind and lame people were considered sinners because it was believed that they or their parents committed some sin that brought on this condition. They were "faulty" human beings and like all sinners, were not allowed within the Temple. He was often accused of being a "friend of sinners." (Matt 9:11; 11:16–19; Luke 15:2; 7:34; Mark 2:15–17)

Jesus said that he was more comfortable on the "sinner" side of the wall than on the "righteous" side, because he felt there was much pseudo-piety and hypocrisy among the righteous. The net result of his life is that he walked all over that dividing line so often it hardly existed for him or his disciples. He thoroughly bewildered the religious hierarchy who were so passionate about keeping that dividing line intact. That may be the most dramatic accomplishment of his earthly life. He didn't believe such dividing lines were helpful or godly. They divide people, making some feel resentful about themselves and others feel self-righteous and smug.

"Those who are well have no need of a physician, but those who are sick. . . For I have come to call not the righteous but sinners." (Matt 9:12–13)

And yet, Christians today frequently divide the world between the lost and the saved, similar to first-century Jews, and one wonders whether Jesus wouldn't be "all over this line," finding among the lost many wonderful, compassionate and generous human beings and among the saved many racists, bigots, sexists and hypocrites.

33. Borg, *Jesus, Uncovering the Life, Teachings and Relevance of a Religious Revolutionary*, 6–7.

Of course, with Paul, "all have sinned and fall short of the glory of God." (Rom 3:23) No question about that.

For me, a "sinner" is someone whose face is turned away from God and away from justice and compassion. One who sells, exploits and oppresses fellow human beings has turned away from God and away from justice and compassion. Such a person is devoted to sin. A person who turns away from a neighbor in need, has turned away from God and away from justice and compassion. A person who is utterly self-absorbed, looking out only for their personal well-being while ignoring the plight of others, has turned away from God and away from justice and compassion. A person who has stiff judgments against those who are different, whether through race, religion, lifestyle, orientation, or nationality, this is a person who has turned away from God and away from justice and compassion.

Let me use my ninety-nine year old mother as an example. Does she sin? It's a foolish question. Of course, she sins. But the Apostle Paul uses the word "saint" to describe the followers of Jesus. And my mother is one of the saints. Not perfect. Not without blemish. But ever since her childhood, she has turned toward God and her savior, Jesus Christ. To call her a sinner would be to major in minors. She has taken some strong stands in her day away from rigid fundamentalism and toward a more tolerant, accepting, less judgmental style of faith. My mother's face has been turned toward God. She has been a writer, an inventor, a volunteer missionary in the USA, the Caribbean and in Africa, and most of all one of the most gracious and hospitable persons I have ever known. "Sinner" isn't the word I would use to describe her ninety-nine years.

For my mother, and for countless others, Jesus' death and resurrection put "sin" behind us. (Rom 6:5–11) Not that we don't commit individual sins, but we have received the forgiving love of God in Christ. Sin is no longer determinative of our lives. It no longer holds sway over us. Sure, we can be disappointed with ourselves. We participate in sinful systems without being aware. We make mistakes. But we live in trust that we are forgiven, and therefore, freed, to live in Christ — without deserving one bit of it. (Eph 2:8) That's grace. We are children of God. We are God's own. In this regard, we aren't unlike other human beings, all of whom are children of God. There's only one difference: some recognize this and embrace it while others do not. Maybe they haven't had the chance. Maybe they purposefully turned away. Maybe we turned them away.

I've heard my mother tell this story about me several times, but in a recently-discovered diary, I read the story as it happened. It was the summer of 1952, and I had not yet turned four. "Steve and Hal got in a fight outdoors and Hal started screaming so I went out to see what it was all about. I asked

Steve if he did anything to Hal and he said no. Then I said, "Now, Steve, are you sure?" He looked at me a minute, then asked, "Was you there all the time?" I told him I wasn't, so, he answered, "Well, then, I didn't do anything to him, but I won't do it anymore!"

We not only want to claim that Jesus was sinless, but we'd prefer to claim the same about ourselves. We don't like to admit mistakes or errors of judgment. And apparently I had this figured out before I was four years old!

Beyond saying, "We are all sinners," I think it is truer to the victory of Christ on the cross to repeat what Jesus said, "I came that they may have life, and have it abundantly." (John 10:10b) *Just as the earthly Jesus put sin behind him by constantly forgiving people of their sins, by preaching forgiveness of sins, by embracing those called "sinners," so does the Risen Christ offer forgiveness and embrace of all human beings as they turn toward him.*

Paul preferred to call believers in Christ, saints, not sinners. "To all the saints in Christ Jesus in Philippi. . ." (Phil 1:1b) "To the saints who are in Ephesus. . ." (1:1b) "To the church of God that is Corinth, including all the saints throughout Achaia. . ." (2 Cor 1:1b) "To the church that is in Corinth, . . .called to be saints. . ." (I Cor 1:2) "To all God's beloved in Rome, who are called to be saints. . ." (Rom 1:7) "To the saints. . .in Christ in Colossae. . ." (Col 1:2)

I'd rather be called a saint, wouldn't you? Particularly if saint doesn't refer to pious perfection, but rather human followers who have purposefully turned toward Jesus to reflect his love.

Are you a sinner or a saint?

Even the most notorious, violent persons can turn to Christ, receive forgiveness, and have their "sins be washed clean." They might still have to pay the consequences for what they have done, just as Zacchaeus did when he repaid all those whom he had cheated as Jericho's tax collector.

Sin is wrong, whether it be in human trafficking, racial prejudice, bullying or domestic violence or mistreating of women, homosexuals, children, the disabled, it's wrong. And we should never go soft on sin. We have a prophetic role in a world filled with sin.

But, in Christ, what we offer isn't a sinless life, but rather a life seeking fulfillment, wholeness, completeness and joy—in others words, shalom.

Jesus died for my sins. I know what it means. I don't argue with it. But what means more to me is that Jesus died that I might enjoy the abundant life (John 10:10b), that I might know victory over death, that I might, through him, experience God's shalom at the heart of my being. And nothing can take that away, not death and not sin. Nothing can separate me from the love of God through Christ Jesus.

If Jesus can prevail over the cross and the tomb, then ultimately the victory belongs to all of us who turn to him for hope, for life, and for joy! Stated negatively, Jesus died so we may overcome our sins. Stated positively, Jesus' death and resurrection offer abundant life, life everlasting.

What difference did Jesus' death and resurrection make? Isn't this the most profound question? Try answering it yourself before you read my list. Jesus died and was resurrected to. . .

1. . . .offer life everlasting. There is no longer reason to fear death. God is victorious over death. The power of death is broken.

2. . . .declare that God ultimately prevails, no matter how rotten the circumstances. God holds the Final Word.

3. . . .offer us hope for today and tomorrow.

4. . . .declare that God can transform any evil into good.

5. . . .represent the Suffering Love of God before all humanity.

6. . . .bring alive the redeeming Spirit of Christ throughout the world for all the ages.

7. . . .offer Eternal Life on earth, in the Here and Now. Eternal life begins now.

8. . . .affirm that God's "YES" is stronger than our "NO"

9. . . .serve as the clearest window to a Loving and Revealed God; to show what Agape Love looks like

10. . . .show that God's love has no boundaries, no limits, not even death.

We can get ourselves so twisted out of shape over unnecessary questions such as, "Did Jesus ever sin?" The question isn't helpful because the answer isn't relevant. It is like asking, "Do you know the way to Tallahassee?," when you don't intend to go there.

That isn't the question. The real question is: what hope does Jesus' death and resurrection offer me? How does my life flourish through him?

The Main Event

I was raised on the Apostle Paul. I knew the stories and parables of Jesus, but they weren't the "main course." Paul was the main course. It is almost assured that we know more about Jesus' years on earth than Paul knew.

Bornkamm wrote, years ago, "One may confidently affirm what many may find surprising and a paradox, that in spite of the almost two thousand years' interval, we today probably know more about the Jesus of history than did Paul."[34] According to Victor Paul Furnish, "It is striking. . .how little use the apostle (Paul) actually makes of Jesus' teachings. . . Paul focuses his attention neither on the teachings of Jesus nor on Jesus' Palestinian ministry. His attention is focused, rather, on Jesus the crucified Messiah and the risen Lord."[35] For Paul, Jesus' death on the cross and his resurrection is enough. You don't need to know anything more. In Paul's view, the way Jesus lived his life on earth mattered far less than the way he suffered, died and was resurrected. Built upon Paul, our faith today is centered upon the cross and the empty tomb.

Jesus' death was his defining moment.

The "main event" in Jesus' life ironically surrounded his death. There is a reason why we "tune-in" to Jesus at the time of his "turning toward Jerusalem," his trials, suffering and death, and follow him through his resurrection.

For Paul, incarnation happened on the cross and in the empty tomb. When Paul writes, "God was in Christ" (2 Co. 5:19), he is speaking of Christ's death and resurrection. Paul believed in the pre-existent Christ who was at the right side of God since the creation of the world. But he largely jumped over Jesus' birth, his ministry, miracles, and parables to place the emphasis of God's salvific activity in Jesus' suffering on the cross and his victory through the empty tomb.

"For I handed on to you as of first importance what I in turn had received: that Christ died. . ." I Corinthians 15:3a

When, for Paul, did Jesus become "the Christ"? When, for Paul, did Jesus become the incarnation of God? When did he become Lord and Savior? We actually don't know the answer to those questions. But by the way Paul "skipped over" the earthly life and ministry of Jesus, Paul emphasized the incarnational power of the cross and empty tomb.

In one approach to Christology, Jesus grew to occupy the role of the Son of God as his life progressed toward the cross. Perhaps his own uncertainty is the reason he deflected so many early questions in the Synoptics about his identity and his role in God's plan. Perhaps that is why he preferred to use the enigmatic term, "Son of Man." The cross and empty tomb

---

34. Bornkamm, *Paul*, 138.
35. Furnish, *Jesus According to Paul*, 40.

are the defining moments which most Christians believe have everything to do with our salvation.

Ask yourself: If Jesus hadn't died on the cross, would he still be our Lord and Savior? If Jesus had died in old age of natural causes, would we be his followers today?

Jesus' Incarnational Journey

Can we speak of Jesus' *Incarnational Journey*, which started with a more limited, youthful understanding but expanded as he approached the end of his life? At that point, Jesus had the understanding and the courage to articulate his Son of Man Prophecies and comprehend what God was calling him to do.

This prophecy, in all its versions, isn't told until mid-way through each of the Synoptic Gospels when "Jesus turned toward Jerusalem." (Luke 9:51) And it is repeated multiple times[36]. Jesus' parables are taught to the crowds, but this is a private prophecy told only to his innermost circle. The fact that Jesus didn't reveal this teaching until late into his ministry suggests that this was a significant learning which he had to "live into" and accept. Who could casually predict that their forthcoming death would be filled with rejection, torture and betrayal? It had to be a journey of courage and understanding, the most significant learning of his unfolding life.

As an expression, "Son of Man" is used only by Jesus and by no one else in the Synoptic Gospels. Jesus said, "The Son of Man must undergo great suffering, and be rejected by the elders, chief priests, and scribes, and be killed, and on the third day be raised." (Luke 9:22) As stated above, this prophecy, which essentially tells "the rest of his story," isn't mentioned in the Synoptic Gospels until mid-point. The fact that it is repeated four to five times in each of these Gospels is a literary method to stress its significance. This prophecy reads into Jesus' life his *teleios*, his destiny. Jesus realized, at this controversial mid-point, where things were headed. Martin Luther King, Jr., also knew at mid-point, that he would likely become a martyr. When Jesus began telling his disciples his Son of Man Prophecy, they were completely befuddled and unprepared for this new teaching.

When did Jesus understand that:

---

36. Five times in Matthew: 16:21–23; 17:12; 17:22–23; 20:17–19; 26:2. Four times in Mark: 8:31–33; 9:12; 9:30–31; 10:32–34; Four times in Luke: 9:22; 9:44–45; 17:24–25; 18:31–34.

- in dying on the cross and overcoming death he would stand as the incarnation of God to all who entered into his death?

- his victory over death would be a victory for everyone who accepts his resurrection?

- he embodied on the cross the self-giving nature of God's agape love?

- when countless millions view his death, which he did nothing to deserve, he would reveal God's awesome love to the world?

- his death and resurrection would become one of the single-most important events in world history?

How can we answer these questions? They require that we know Jesus' self-understanding of his death and resurrection. And what about the understanding of his first followers? They did not know the meaning of the cross and empty tomb prior to their experience of it. The Gospels report that his disciples were befuddled by his Son of Man prophecies. Thus, the church grew in its understanding of the incarnation. No one expanded that understanding more than the Apostle Paul, some twenty years later. The church itself was on an "Incarnational Journey" that came to fruition after the New Testament was written. James G.B. Dunn wrote in the acclaimed Anchor Bible Dictionary: ". . .it is doubtful whether the concept (of incarnation) in such a developed sense can be found anywhere within the Bible, since clearly presupposed therein is the full-blown Trinitarian doctrine as that came to expression in the 4th and 5th centuries of the Christian era." (p. 397—398) "Is the word 'incarnation' appropriate to describe Jesus' self-consciousness or claims he made regarding himself? (p. 400) ". . .there is nothing of consequence to support the thesis that Jesus saw himself in some sense as God, the incarnation of deity. . . .It is unlikely. . .that the thought of incarnation was part of the earliest Christian faith, or that the conviction regarding Jesus' exaltation to God's right hand would have seen more or less from the first to carry that corollary within it."[37] There are certainly seeds of an incarnational theology in the Synoptic Gospels (e.g., Matt 11:27—28), further developed in the Gospel of John and in Paul. And these seeds took root in the church and came to fuller expression a few centuries later. The Incarnational Journey, beginning with Jesus, continued.

It is a salvific journey not only down through history, but also a journey in which each of us must embark. If we do not understand incarnation, we do not understand the cross or the empty tomb. Nor can we fully embrace the Good News of Jesus Christ.

37. Dunn, Anchor Bible Dictionary, Vol. 3, 397–398, 400, 401.

Paul repeats this message so often in his writings. In his seminal theological writing in Romans, Paul claims:

"For while we were still weak, at the right time Christ died for the ungodly." (5:6)

". . .God proves his love for us in that while we still were sinners Christ died for us." (5:8)

". . .all of us who have been baptized into Christ Jesus were baptized into his death. Therefore, we have been buried with him by baptism into death, so that, just as Christ was raised from the dead by the glory of the Father, so we too might walk in newness of life." (6:3b-4)

"For if we have been united with him in a death like his, we will certainly be united with him in a resurrection like his. We know that our old self was crucified with him so that the body of sin might be destroyed, and we might no longer be enslaved to sin. . . But if we have died with Christ, we believe that we will also live with him. We know that Christ, being raised from the dead, will never die again; death no longer has dominion over him." (6:5-9)

"It is Christ Jesus, who died, yes, who was raised, who is at the right hand of God, who indeed intercedes for us." (8:34)

". . .to this end Christ died and lived again, so that he might be Lord of both the dead and the living." (14:9)

Where are you on an "incarnational journey?

SETTLED FAITH

If Jesus was born omniscient, if he already possessed full wisdom, if as an infant he possessed the answer to every question, then he is a model of Settled Faith. He was stationary and fixed upon God's righteousness. His life was settled from the beginning and there was no need for him to discover, stretch, or learn. He was filled with certitude. He was an "Arrived Jesus."

SEEKING FAITH

If Jesus was born into this world as a human baby, born into a household convinced he held a special destiny from God, if in his growing years he became increasingly convinced of God's call, if early in life he seemed gifted and suited for that calling—then there was a steep learning curve ahead of him to fulfill the special role in human history God intended. He possessed a thriving, questioning, seeking spirit with an amazing appetite for learning. Nothing less would serve God's call. He was a "Becoming Jesus."

Why is this important? Because for too many Christians, faith is settled, beliefs are concretized, values are frozen and satisfaction with the way things are is the norm. The reputation of Christians in wider society is that

...we are rigid,

...our minds are made up,

...we are "the convinced,"

...we have nothing more to learn,

...our faith is firmly rooted and "we shall not be moved,"

...we embody Settled Faith, and

...we are Captains of Certainty.

Outside the church, many people look at us and are convinced that we believe we are filled with God's omniscience. We come off as closed-minded know-it-alls. We already possess the truth of our salvation and we need nothing more.

In poll after poll, when the attitudes of Christians are considered, we generally linger behind society on nearly every issue. To my mind, we are often the last to recognize the liberating work of Christ in the world around us. And we communicate that we are stuck in the past, unwilling to consider our God who is "making all things new."

In my church growing up, we recognized two categories of people:

The Reached and the Unreached.

It was much like the Jews of the first century who divided their world between the Righteous and Sinners. The sole purpose of the Reached was to try to convince the Unreached to "cross over." It wasn't until later in my life that I discovered that I didn't fit comfortably in either category. I wasn't fully Reached because there were too many unredeemed parts of my life. God wasn't finished with me yet (and still isn't). Yet, I wasn't among "the Unreached" either.

I discovered another category of people, *"the Reaching."* These are people who have experienced God's love to the point that they want more—but neither have they arrived. They haven't yet allowed God's Holy Spirit to reach into every crevice of their being. The Reaching are on their way—on God's way. The reaching are those who "give all they know of themselves to all they know of God." But we are constantly learning more of ourselves and therefore more of God. Too many Christians today believe that they belong to "the Reached" and therefore no more work, struggle, or self-reflection are needed. It's harder to be among the Reaching, but its far closer to what the apostle Paul taught and what Jesus lived.

Where are you: among the reached, the unreached,
or the reaching?

Life-Long Learners

If we come to understand Jesus as a life-long learner, as one reaching for the high call that God intended for him, then perhaps more of his followers today would also seek to be life-long learners. Yet, the state of learning in the church today is abysmal. In many churches, only a handful of adults are engaged in organized learning. In many churches, classes and preachers merely repeat what is already known. They re-inforce—they do not stretch. Rarely is a new thought considered. In many churches, *learning is threatening*. Learning requires that we go beyond certainty, beyond absolute confidence, and beyond complacency. Learning requires that we ask questions and follow a quest toward new insight. If we are learning, then our faith cannot be settled. And that is a threatening insight for many Christians.

In your experience, is learning threatening within the church?

There needs to be a *Learning Reformation* in the church today. There has to be some forum, some avenue within the church, where we can reflect together on what God is doing in our world, in our lives, and in the church. There has to be some place where we can honestly try to make sense of our experience. This involves learning. We need more congregations of seeking adults, youth and children actively forming and reforming their faith throughout their life pilgrimage. It would be a community of people unafraid of questions. It would be a community whose idea of God is big enough to respond to life's most sincere questions and deepest doubts. It would be a community convinced that God will be where our questions lead. And it begins by our developing a vision of a Learning Jesus.

How many people have been driven from the church because they accepted a Settled Faith, and when they encountered a crisis, their faith was woefully ill-prepared to respond? The "easy answers" couldn't address the absurdities of life.

One morning I was in a men's Bible class and one of the participants said, "My participation in this church has been like enrolling in a university. I have learned so much from all my interactions here, unlike other churches to which I have belonged. My understanding of the Bible is now much more than ever before and some of the assumptions I held upon coming into this church have been shaken. And that's good." He is a follower of a Learning Jesus!

We do not insult Jesus with the idea that he grew into God's calling, and that learning was crucial to his spiritual journey. Neither do we diminish Jesus by accepting his humanity. Rather, we elevate his role as a learning model for all who follow him. Indeed, let's celebrate that Jesus was one of the most fascinating learners in all human history!

We have stunted our spiritual formation by believing in an "arrived Jesus" rather than a "becoming Jesus." We have even thought of ourselves as having "arrived" rather than as "becoming."

We follow our Lord and Savior who had a huge appetite for life, an insatiable desire to learn about God's call and destiny, an intense longing to grow into all that God was calling him to be. We follow the Learning Jesus.

Chapter Three

Learning Jesus

"That is not the way you learned Christ!"

EPHESIANS 4:20

Apostle Paul's language may not point us in the right direction. He speaks often of "believing" in Christ. As if a doctrinal assent, a belief in Christ, is all that is involved. Yet, Paul would be the first to say that "right belief" does not express what following the Living Christ involves.

Marcus Borg helps us understand how our modern language can get in the way of understanding what Paul had in mind. Borg maintains, ". . .in the last four hundred years or so, the word 'believe' has undergone a radical change of meaning, so that it's modern meaning is very different from its premodern meanings. For most modern Christians, believing means believing a set of claims, a set of statements: believing that God exists, that the Bible is the Word of God, that Jesus is the Son of God, that he was born of a virgin, that he died for our sins, that he rose from the dead, that he is the only way of salvation, that he will come again, and so forth. This is believing as affirming a set of beliefs to be true.

"But prior to about the year 1600, the verb 'believe' had a very different meaning within Christianity as well as in popular usage. It did not mean believing statements to be true; the object of the verb 'believe' was always a person, not a statement. This is the difference between *believing that* and *believing in*. To believe *in* a person is quite different from believing *that* a series of statements about the person are true. In premodern English, be-lieving meant *believing in* and thus a relationship of trust, loyalty, and love. Most simply, to believe meant to belove. . . to 'believe' meant to commit one's allegiance, loyalty, and love to God and Jesus. . . *Believing that* and *believing in* are very different. The first leads to an emphasis on correct belief, on believing the right things. The second leads to a transformed life."[1]

Harvey Cox wrote, "We have been misled for many centuries by the theologians who taught that 'faith' consisted in dutifully believing the ar-ticles listed in one of the countless creeds they have spun out. But it does not. . . Once I realized that Christianity is not a creed and that faith is more a matter of embodiment than of axioms, things changed."[2]

What's wrong when we view Christianity as a set of beliefs about . . . ?

Every time Paul wrote of believing, he meant to *believe in Christ*. The Judeo-Christian faith comes down to relationships. Often, Chris-tians maintain that the Jews are bound to a rigid external Law while Christians are free in the Spirit. There were historical periods when the Jews became legalistic—treating faith as if an external allegiance to a written code. But that is not the Jewish faith at its highest and best. Through Ezekiel, God said, "I will remove from your body the heart of stone and give you a heart of flesh. I will put my spirit within you. . ." (36:26—27a) And what is that Heart of Stone but the Ten Command-ments etched in stone brought down off the mountain by Moses? It never has been enough to follow the code, or even abide by the Torah as an external set of commandments. The Torah must be internalized, taken inside our hearts, and lived out in relationship with the Living God. That is why, at every twist and turn of Hebrew Scripture, it is rela-tionship with the Living God that truly counts. The Torah is but a sign that a Jew is in a living, dynamic relationship with God. Jeremiah wrote, "But this is the covenant that I will make with the house of Israel after those days, says the Lord: I will put my law within them, and I will write on their hearts; and I will be their God, and they shall be my people." (Jer 31:33) Jesus summarized the Jewish faith by saying, "You shall love the Lord your God with all your heart, and with all your soul, and with all your strength, and with all your mind. . ." (Luke 10:27) It must be internalized.

1. Borg, *Jesus, Uncovering the Life, Teachings and Relevance of a Religious Revolu-tionary,* 20–21.

2. Cox, *The Future of Faith,* 18–19.

Do you view Judaism as a set of commandments, or a covenant of relationship with God?

I am convinced that Jesus did not intend to start a new religion, separate from Judaism. Or that the two would, at far too many times in history, experience alienation and hostility. That was not his calling or intent.

The Hebrew Scriptures hold together a tension between two traditions. The first is the particular tradition, in which God came to the Jews, blessed them, and called them as a people. If you follow this tradition too closely, then Yahweh is the God of the Jews, just as the Persians had their god and the Egyptians had theirs. God becomes a nationalistic god.

There is another tradition in Hebrew Scripture which counters this exclusive claim, and it is the universalist tradition. In this, God came to the Jews, called them to be a people in order to introduce the God of Heaven and Earth to all the nations. Yahweh is not just another nationalist god, but the Only God. The particular tradition, identifying God as the God of Israel, is the dominant voice. But the universalist tradition is persistent: the Jews haven't been blessed as much as called. They are the conduit through which monotheism is introduced to the world. And no Jew in history stands in this broader tradition more than Jesus of Nazareth.

It was the universal voice that resonated so well throughout the Roman world. Weary of their nationalistic gods laden with self-serving and even hedonistic images, the Jewish universal, monotheistic voice attracted Gentiles far and wide. In the first century, it was truly an alternative religious voice in a polytheistic world.

That is why there were so many "god-fearers" in synagogues throughout the Roman Empire. These god-fearers were Gentiles who sympathized in every way with the Jewish faith, were faithful to synagogue worship, observed the law as much as possible, carried out acts of justice and good works, and were drawn to the superior ethical teachings and practices of the Jews. But they weren't prepared to leave their own ethnicity behind to *become* a Jew. They were deeply attracted to Judaism, but they did not want to fully "become Jewish" through circumcision. It would mean turning from their ethnic identity. Being Gentiles, many of these god-fearers were well-connected to society and were helpful to Jewish synagogues in Gentile cities around the Empire. Being Jewish in a Gentile city set them apart and it meant that access to power, citizenship, and full societal participation were often limited. God-fearers were a bridge between the synagogue and the larger society.

The Jewish faith in the Roman Empire had done an admirable job attracting Gentiles to their synagogues. They had done a good job standing apart from the syncretic religions throughout the Empire. They offered a clear alternative and many Gentiles responded. But these Gentiles were also second-class members of the synagogue, included but not fully embraced because they had not left behind their Gentile ethnicity and fully entered Judaism. They were prevalent in almost every synagogue throughout the Empire but they were also at an impasse: attracted, but not fully accepted. They were not in the center of the synagogue no matter how active or devoted they had become. They were on the edge. They were separate and unequal.

I recall a similar division in my Baptist church growing up in mid-Missouri. We had twenty or so participants in the church active in every way, but they did not join because they declined to be re-baptized. They felt their original baptism was an authentic expression of their faith journey. They were active in our church, but because they did not want to be re-baptized, they remained on the edge. They were "partly in" and "partly out."

Can you imagine how good this news sounded when Paul un-coupled the universal Jewish message from the ethnic identity of Jews? People could respond to the God of Heaven and Earth and the Author of Salvation without becoming an ethnic Jew. Paul stood in the tradition of Jesus and took it to a world hungry for his inclusive good news. This universal message could no longer be contained by any nationality, ethnicity, or geographical region. "There is no longer Jew or Greek, there is no longer slave or free, there is no longer male or female; for all of you are one in Christ Jesus." (Gal 3:28) "For in Christ Jesus neither circumcision or uncircumcision counts for anything; the only thing that counts is faith working through love." (Gal 5:6) In other words, be a practicing Jew or not, but enter into a relationship with God in Jesus Christ.

Jesus crossed every boundary set before him, constantly pushing his fellow Jews to consider their God as the God of all peoples and nations. His message came down on the inclusive, universal side. He overcame the divisions that their faith had created in the first century: between righteous and sinners, between women and men, between Samaritans and Jews.

Jesus talked about relationship with God. He called God, "Abba," a close, intimate, familial term. (Mark 14:36) The wide, inclusive sweep of his message was not about to stop with the Jews—it was a tide that could not be stopped. And as it began to include Gentiles throughout the Roman world within one generation of his life—it was a sweep too broad for many Jews. Jesus didn't live long enough to confront the question as to whether his followers would need to be circumcised as Jews. Paul took the gospel of Jesus to the Gentile world and the message of Jesus kept broadening. It broke Paul's heart when fellow Jews largely turned against him and could not embrace the inclusive message of Christ.

Jesus believed in the Sabbath. He maintained the Sabbath and as far as we know he never missed observing a Sabbath. He always preached and taught in the synagogues on the Sabbath. But he said, "The Sabbath was made for humankind, and not humankind for the Sabbath." (Mark 2:27) He believed in the spirit of the Sabbath, as it turns us toward God, but not in the regulations regarding the Sabbath, which can become self-serving.

I think his attitude toward circumcision would likely be the same: when possible, maintain the tradition, but the spirit of it has to do with "marking ourselves" in some way to remind ourselves of our allegiance to God. Circumcision per se isn't the point. And our ethnicity isn't the point. Declaring fully and plainly that we follow in Jesus' way is the point.

The Christian Way kept getting broader and more inclusive and nothing could stop it: not circumcision, not the Roman Empire, and not persecution. No boundary could contain the way of Jesus. Paul wrote to the Galatians, ". . .for in Christ Jesus you are all children of God through faith." (3:26) And to the Corinthians, "For in the one Spirit we were all baptized into one body—Jews or Greeks, slaves or free—and we were all made to drink of one Spirit." (I Cor 12:13)

It is easy to recognize the challenge of the broadening Christian movement from the perspective of Antioch. Paul and Barnabas worked there together for eight to nine years, building up the Christian church. There were many godfearers in Antioch connected to the synagogues throughout the city. The questions of circumcision and the observance of the ritual commandments between the godfearers and the Jews in those synagogues seemed not to be of critical importance among the Jews of Antioch, and this in turn gave Christians relative freedom. And thus developed in Antioch the formation of a Christian community separate from the synagogue. The requirements of circumcision and ritual law in the Antioch church were largely ignored. What developed in Antioch was an open table fellowship, agape feast, and Lord's Supper in which there was no distinction between Jew and Gentile, between slave and free, or between women and men. It was a broad and open table fellowship where equality and unity were embodied in their worship and fellowship. Peter freely and openly shared in that inclusive table fellowship.

However, a delegation of Jews from the Jerusalem Church was sent by James (Jesus' brother) because he was concerned that Gentiles were entering the church in Antioch without proper observance of Jewish faith. Suddenly, Peter no longer engaged in this fellowship, but ate only with fellow Jews. And then, even Barnabas was persuaded to discontinue fellowship with

Gentile converts. And finally, most of the Jewish members of the church withdrew. Thus, the broad inclusive table at Antioch was suddenly fractured, with the Jews and Peter and Barnabas withdrawing. Paul wrote, "For until certain people came from James, Peter used to eat with Gentiles. But after they came, he drew back and kept himself separate for fear of the circumcision faction. And the other Jews joined him in this hypocrisy, so that even Barnabas was led astray by their hypocrisy." (Gal 2:12—13)

And now it was not just a living relationship with Jesus Christ that brought the Antioch church together around one table, but other requirements were applied which made the godfearers once again second-class participants. When the Jews in the church would no longer sit in fellowship with the Gentiles, Paul was furious with this sudden about-face that fractured the church. Paul wrote, ". . .for in Christ Jesus you are all children of God through faith. As many of you as were baptized into Christ have clothed yourselves with Christ. There is no longer Jew or Greek. . ." (Gal 3:26–28a)

For Paul, the issue revolved around relationship. Paul would say that we must be "in Christ." We have to enter into Christ, we have to be a part of the Body of Christ, and we have to be a part of Christ's incarnational presence in the world.

We have to learn Christ. Not learn about Christ. Not learn of Christ. But *learn Christ*. Paul expressed it: "That is not the way you learned Christ." (Eph 4:20) Precisely!

How have you learned Jesus?

We have to take Christ within us or nothing else much matters. "Do you not realize that Jesus Christ is in you?" (2 Cor 13:5c) When we take Christ within us, then we truly learn discipleship, sacrifice, generosity, the necessity of suffering, and the need to take the narrow road.

This isn't about externals. It never was—though the Pharisees sometimes acted as if that was what truly mattered. "Woe to you, scribes and Pharisees, hypocrites! For you clean the outside of the cup and of the plate, but inside they are full of greed and self-indulgence." (Matt 23:25) Many Christians also have had their allegiance to externals, to rules. This isn't about externals. It's about a matter of the heart and how the "heart" gets expressed in our lives.

Followers of Christ must learn Christ. Learn him—as in a personal relationship. He matters. Not creeds, not doctrines, not structures, but him.

The challenge of "learning Jesus" is that he didn't conform to the values of his society, nor to ours. When we learn Jesus, we learn values counter to our culture. No human civilization has ever used the Beatitudes as the basis for organizing itself. The spirit of Jesus runs contrary to common sense and often counter to cultural norms. So *Learning Jesus* is learning to respond in ways that run contrary to the dominant cultural values around us.

And that is why learning Jesus is an on-going journey. It isn't accomplished in one conversion experience. I have always been drawn to the call of faith as being "To give all we know of ourselves to all we know of God." *(source unknown)* As a seventh grader, I could give all I knew of myself to all I knew of God, yet that would be a woefully inadequate expression of faith as a young adult, a middle-aged adult, or a senior adult.

We must learn Jesus in community so that we are not misled by the cultural enticements around us. We must learn Jesus throughout our lifetimes so that our assumptions, prejudices and cultural biases are always challenged. Jesus said, "Take my yoke upon you, and learn from me. . ." (Matt 11:29a)

We must learn Jesus as our singular life-long call—until we meet him on the other side. "For now we see in a mirror, dimly, but then we will see face to face. Now I know only in part; then I will know fully, even as I have been fully known." (I Cor 13:12)

Bibliography

Anderson, Galusha. *A Border City During the Civil War*. Colonial, 1908.

Barclay, William. *The Gospel of Luke, The Daily Study Bible Series*. Westminster Press, 1956.

Berger, Peter. *Christian Century Magazine*. 1997.

Bornkamm, Gunther. *Paul*. Harper and Row, 1969.

Borg, Marcus. *Jesus, Uncovering the Life, Teachings and Relevance of a Religious Revolutionary*. Harper, San Francisco, 2006

Brooks, David. *New York Times, OpEd*. April 15, 2016.

Buechner, Frederick. *The Sacred Journey*. Harper and Row, 1982.

Chittister, Joan. *Scarred by Struggle, Transformed by Hope*. Eerdmans, 2003.

Christian Century Magazine, March 15, 2017, quoting *The Washington Post*.

Cox, Harvey. *The Future of Faith*. Harper One, 2009.

Culpepper, R. Alan. *The Gospel of Luke, The New Interpreter's Bible*. Volume IX, Abingdon Press, 1995.

Dear, John. *The Questions of Jesus*. Penguin, Random House, 2004.

Enns, Peter. *The Sin of Certainty, Why God Desires Our Trust More Than Our 'Correct' Beliefs*. Harper One, 2017.

Ehrman, Bart D., trans. *The Infancy Gospel of Thomas*. In *Lost Scriptures, Books That Did Not Make It Into the New Testament*. Oxford, 2003.

Furnish, Victor Paul. *Jesus According to Paul*. Cambridge, 1993.

Gillman, Florence Morgan. *Anchor Bible Dictionary*. Vol. 3, Doubleday, 1992.

Griffin, Emelie. *Turning, Reflections on the Experience of Conversion*. Doubleday, 1980.

Gushee, David. *Still Christian, Following Jesus Out of American Evangelicalism*. Westminster John Knox, 2017.

Interpreter's Dictionary of the Bible. Abingdon, 1962.

Jones, Stephen D. *Peaceteacher, Jesus' Way of Shalom*. Trafford/Baptist Peace Fellowship of North America, 2011.

———. *Rabbi Jesus, Learning from the Master Teacher*. Peake Road/Smyth and Helwys, Macon, Georgia, 1997.

Nouwen, Henri. *Turn My Mourning into Dancing*. Thomas Nelson, 2001

———. *With Open Hands*, Ballantine, 1972.

Palmer, Parker J. *The Courage to Teach,* Jossey-Bass, 1998.

Pekar, Thaler. "Certainty versus Confidence." *Stanford Social Innovation Review,* January 11, 2013.

Robinson, James M. *The Gospel of Jesus.* Harper, 2005.

Robinson, John A. T. *The Human Face of God.* Westminster, 1973.

VentureBlog. April 10, 2008.

Weems, Renita. *Listening for God: A Minister's Journey through Silence and Doubt.* Touchstone, 1999.

Westerhoff, John H., III. *Will Our Children Have Faith?* Seabury, New York, 1976.